Learn BOOKKEEPING in 7 DAYS

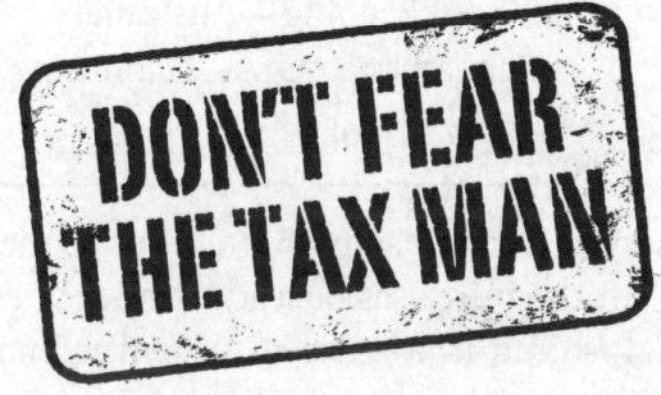

ROD CALDWELL

First published 2010 by Wrightbooks
an imprint of John Wiley & Sons Australia, Ltd
42 McDougall Street, Milton Qld 4064

Office also in Melbourne

Typeset in Berkley LT 11.3/14pt

National Library of Australia Cataloguing-in-Publication data:

Author:	Caldwell, Rod.
Title:	Learn bookkeeping in 7 days: don't fear the tax man / Rod Caldwell.
ISBN:	9781742469539 (pbk.)
Notes:	Includes index.
Subjects:	Bookkeeping—Australia. Small business—Accounting.
Dewey number:	657.20994

Cover design by Xou Creative

Printed in Australia by McPherson's Printing Group

10 9 8 7 6 5 4 3 2 1

Disclaimer

The material in this publication is of the nature of general comment only, and does not represent professional advice. It is not intended to provide specific guidance for particular circumstances and it should not be relied on as the basis for any decision to take action or not take action on any matter which it covers. Readers should obtain professional advice where appropriate, before making any such decision. To the maximum extent permitted by law, the author and publisher disclaim all responsibility and liability to any person, arising directly or indirectly from any person taking or not taking action based upon the information in this publication.

Contents

About the author

Rod Caldwell is a tax accountant by profession and a TAFE business lecturer by choice. He worked for the Australian Taxation Office (ATO) for 20 years before leaving in 2005 to start a new career as a lecturer in business studies at a Perth technical college. Rod has a bachelor of commerce degree from the University of Western Australia and a postgraduate diploma in advanced taxation from the University of New South Wales. Rod is also a Fellow of CPA Australia.

This book was written as a direct result of his involvement with small business owners through the Adult and Community Education courses he delivers in Western Australia.

Additional resources are available from the author's website <www.tpabusiness.com.au>. The author can be contacted by email at <rod@tpabusiness.com.au>. All comments from the readers of this book, students or lecturers are welcome.

Preface

Who should read this book?

This book is aimed squarely at the small business operator, often a home-based business, with an annual turnover of less than $2 million. Why less than $2 million? Because that is what the Australian Taxation Office (ATO) uses to define a small business entity that can use cash accounting methods for the purposes of calculating its goods and services tax (GST) and income tax liability. Small businesses with a turnover in excess of $2 million but less than $20 million, classified as small to medium enterprises (SMEs), are required to use accrual accounting, both for Tax Office purposes and to conform with Australian accounting standards. As the concept of accrual accounting is covered in this book, SME operators will also find this book an invaluable resource.

What will I learn?

This book will teach you how to keep cash-based manual accounting records that satisfy your needs for the calculation of your quarterly GST liability and can also be used by your accountant when preparing your annual income tax return. Helpful examples are included, along with useful exercises, all accompanied by a full worked solution. Each exercise has its own set of blank forms, formatted specifically for the requirements of that task. A full set can also be downloaded from my website <www.tpabusiness.com.au>.

This book as a lecturer's resource

If you are intending to use this book for a nonaccredited introduction to bookkeeping course, the duration of which is most likely to be six weeks, the seven-day structure that I have designed can still be organised into a six-session module according to your students' needs. Since most students will not be purchasing inventory or making sales on credit terms, the topics discussed under day 5 can be referred to in passing and the material in day 7 can form the basis of your final class. On the other hand, if you have students who need to know how to account for credit purchases and sales, then include day 5 in your course and explain that the material covered under day 7 is for additional reading after the course is completed.

Additional resources such as PDF versions of the exercise solutions and an online computer-based learning tool are available on my website <www.tpabusiness.com.au>.

Rod Caldwell
Perth
March 2010

Day 1

Introduction to bookkeeping and accounting

Key terms and concepts

- *Small business:* defined by the Australian Taxation Office (ATO) as a business with an annual turnover of less than $2 million. They are often referred to as micro businesses.
- *General ledger account:* holds the details of business transactions of the same type.
- *Debit:* an entry in a general ledger account that represents the economic inflows from a business transaction.
- *Credit:* an entry in a general ledger account that represents the economic outflows from a business transaction.
- *Chart of accounts:* a numerical index used within general ledger accounts.
- In all business transactions the economic inflows (debit entries) must equal the economic outflows (credit entries).

So that we're all on the same page let's examine the classification structure of business in Australia. The Tax Office defines **small businesses** with a **turnover** of under $2 million per year as small business entities and will often refer to them as **micro businesses**. There are certain taxation concessions available to micro businesses that will be discussed later in this book. Micro businesses usually account for their business **transactions** under Tax Office rules and on a **cash** basis.

Classified next are **small to medium enterprises** (SMEs), also defined by the Tax Office as small businesses, with a turnover in excess of $2 million, and finally large corporate entities, which have a turnover of more than $20 million per year and are often listed on the stock exchange. These enterprises account for their business transactions on an accrual basis under Australian **accounting standards**, but they still use the same **bookkeeping** methods as micro businesses.

This book is written for a small family business, probably run from home, with a turnover, that is, your annual 'business' sales, of less than $2 million. The main taxation concession available to you is that you can calculate your net income for income tax purposes on a cash basis. If you elect to do this, you can also calculate your **goods and services tax (GST)** liability on a cash basis. This book assumes that you have elected to use **cash accounting** for both your income tax and the GST.

It also assumes that your annual turnover exceeds $75 000. If it is less than this amount, you do not have to register for the GST. You can use this book to determine how to keep your records, but ignore the GST information as it will not apply to you.

This book also caters for the SME, the small to medium enterprise, with a turnover in excess of $2 million but less than $20 million per year. As this type of business accounts for its GST and income tax on an accrual basis, the cash accounting sections within this book can be ignored by this business group.

Why keep accounting records?

Accounting is the process of identifying, measuring and communicating economic information to permit informed judgements and decisions by users of the information. In the case of small business, the users are the owners themselves, using the information to determine the profit made. They also use the information to report their GST liability to their accountant via their quarterly **Business Activity Statement (BAS)** and calculate their income tax due on an annual basis.

The accounting system identifies and records business transactions through a mechanism known as **journals** that summarises the information that is then recorded into a set of accounts, based on a system of accounting known as **double-entry bookkeeping**.

Accounting information, once recorded in the set of accounts, is then communicated using financial statements prepared from those accounts. The recording of the accounting information is called bookkeeping, while the interpretation and reporting of that information is called accounting. The boundary between bookkeeping and accounting is usually considered to be the **trial balance**, which is a summary of all information entered into the system over a given period. It is from the trial balance that the financial statements are derived.

The main financial accounting statements

The purpose of financial accounting statements is mainly to show the financial position of a business at a particular point in time and to show how that business has performed over a specific period.

The three main financial accounting statements that help achieve this aim are:

- a **balance sheet** for the business at the end of the reporting period
- the **income statement** for the reporting period
- a **cash flow statement** for the reporting period.

A balance sheet shows at a particular point in time what resources are owned by a business ('**assets**') and what it owes to other parties ('liabilities'). It also shows how much has been invested in the business and what the sources of that investment finance were. It is often helpful to think of a balance sheet as a 'snapshot' of the business—a picture of the financial position of the business at a specific point.

By contrast, the income statement (or **profit and loss statement** as it is also known) provides a perspective for a longer time period. It is the story of what financial transactions took place in a particular period—and (most importantly) what the overall result of those transactions was. Not surprisingly, the profit and loss statement measures 'profit'. Profit is the amount by which **sales revenue** (also known as 'turnover' or 'income') exceeds 'expenses' (or 'costs') for the period being measured.

The third report, the cash flow statement, reveals details of the source of the business cash inflows and where it expended its cash outflows. Its primary purpose is to provide the reader with details of the liquidity of the business. Further discussion of this statement is beyond the scope of this book.

Accounting versus bookkeeping

Bookkeeping is the processes involved in the 'correct' recording of your business transactions. Accounting is the processes involved in taking that information and creating the financial reports. The division between the two lies at the trial balance.

All processes involved up to the trial balance stage, including your bank reconciliation statement and BAS preparation, could be considered to be bookkeeping. The process of taking that trial balance and modifying the figures to meet accounting standards and then producing your balance sheet and income statement, including your income tax return, is considered to be accounting.

This book limits itself to bookkeeping, that is, the recording of accounting information, its verification through the bank reconciliation process to the trial balance and preparation of your quarterly BAS.

The accounting framework

The theory of accounting has developed the concept of a 'true and fair view'. The true and fair view is a concept that is applied to ensure that your accounts do indeed accurately portray your business activities. Under this concept you should record your business transactions as they truly are and not try to bend the rules to suit your own purposes.

To support the application of the true and fair view, accounting has adopted certain conventions and concepts which help to ensure that accounting information is presented accurately and consistently.

The above discussion is all very well from an academic viewpoint, but from the view of a small business, accounting records are mainly held to satisfy the Tax Office, both for GST and for income tax. However, proper accounting can also be a source of management information that can help your business grow. The timely analysis of your trading activities by comparison against your business plan, operational budget and projected cash flows can help you foresee and correct any problems that may arise before they can adversely affect your business activities.

Small business should aim at completing management tasks with as little effort as possible. But that does not necessarily mean that you do not wish to do it correctly, just as efficiently as possible and to get it right the first time.

The accounting conventions that are most important in this book are:

- *monetary*. All accounting transactions are expressed in dollar terms.
- *entity*. You and your business are two separate entities (unlike at law).
- *periodic*. Your accounting records are divided into periods—usually monthly, quarterly and annually.

Only monetary transactions that lead to you having a legal obligation to pay or receive money, or money equivalent (as in barter), are recorded in your accounting system. The fact that you, as the owner, have particular skills in running a business or, on the contrary, are a complete novice, is not recorded. This should be borne in mind when purchasing a business or **franchise** with a purchase price based upon the financial statements.

Every business should start by opening a cheque account with a bank. From the viewpoint of accounting, that bank account is your business. You should not mix any personal monies with your business funds. Your business and you are considered to be two completely separate entities. This is different from the legal (and taxable) position where you are the business. Your business has a financial life of its own; it owns assets and makes transactions. From the perspective of accounting, you are simply its servant. The legal perspective is somewhat more complex.

Your accounting cycle will be based upon the tax year, and further broken down into months. This is so that you can reconcile your bank account to your books on a monthly basis. To facilitate this you should arrange for your bank to send you a monthly **bank statement** (either by post or electronically).

Your financial year will start on 1 July and end on 30 June (the same as your tax year). You will record all of your transactions weekly and transfer them to your **general ledger** (post them) in monthly 'batches' and check your balances against your bank statement (a bank reconciliation). You will then complete your BAS on a quarterly basis. Bookkeeping is cyclical, weekly, monthly, quarterly and, finally, annual. Each year is discrete, that is you start from a zero point as of 1 July each year.

How to set up a business

Your first task when you decide to start a business is to consider which entity type you are going to use. Each type has different accounting requirements and taxation implications, although *all* have the same bookkeeping basis. In this book our focus is on manual bookkeeping to the trial balance stage. All business entities share the same path to the trial balance. It is the accounting stage that comes after the trial balance, that is, how the profit or loss is accounted for, distributed and taxed, that will differ for each business type.

There are three main business types, with a fourth tax-specific type:

- *sole trader*. Just you running the whole show
- *partnership*. Often small businesses are run as husband-and-wife partnerships

- *company*. A private company (Pty Ltd) registered with the Australian Securities and Investments Commission (ASIC)
- *family trust*. A tax-effective method of doing business that is beyond the scope of this book.

Note

In this book we will consider only the bookkeeping requirements of a sole trader. The bookkeeping arrangements for a partnership, company or trust are for all practical purposes identical, but the accounting functions, that is, the post-trial balance adjustments, do contain marked differences from the process used for the sole trader. We will be concentrating on cash accounting. 'Accrual' accounting refers to the concept of matching revenue with the appropriate expenditure and requires, among other things, end-of-year adjustments for prepaid expenses or revenues received but not yet earned. Such adjustments are accounting functions and are beyond the scope of this text.

Each business type has different legal requirements. However, you can start a small business as a **sole trader** without any formal 'legal' requirements. A **partnership** likewise can be commenced between two persons, usually husband and wife, with no more than a joint business bank account to prove their intention, although some form of written agreement, called a **partnership agreement**, would be considered prudent.

A **company** or a trust must be set up by your accountant and requires formal legal involvement and additional costs.

After determining your business type, you can then set up the business structure:

- Register your **trading name** with the Department of Consumer & Employment Protection.
- Register your business with the **ATO** using your trading name and obtain an **Australian Business Number (ABN).**
- Open a business bank account—your cheques will show your ABN and trading name. Make sure that your bank provides you with monthly bank statements.

Note

If the address of your business is your home address, you may wish to check with the local council about any restrictions on home-based businesses in your area.

All of the above can be arranged by yourself, especially if you are entering into a sole trader or family partnership, but it would be wise at this stage to consult your accountant to ensure that you have all the bases covered.

Tax and the small business

As a sole trader, you will be taxed on your business activities under the GST and income tax. Your business net income will be added to your other sources of income and you will pay income tax based upon the total amount. A detailed discussion of income tax and the BAS are beyond the scope of this book; however, the correct accounting of your business transactions to the trial balance stage will provide the basic information required to calculate the amounts owing for both of these taxes. For details on the calculation of your quarterly GST liability, see day 6.

If your business has an expected turnover of less than $75 000, you don't have to register for the GST. The downside is that you can't claim any GST credits. In tax terms you will be 'input' taxed, which means that you will be taxed on your inputs but not on your sales.

If your annual turnover is expected to be less than $2 million, you can account for both your GST liability and your income tax liability on a cash basis. This book assumes that you are a sole trader with a business that falls into the $75 000 to $2 million bracket and that you wish to account on a cash basis.

Your BAS will usually be processed quarterly and is most likely completed by the business proprietor (yourself) and reviewed by your accountant on an annual basis. Your income tax requirements are usually undertaken by your accountant on an annual basis.

Transactions: debits and credits

All business activity involves transactions, that is, the buying and selling of something, be it tangible or a service. You buy a pair of shoes; that is a transaction. You provide a service for a fee; that is a transaction. You pay your electricity account; that is a transaction. And all of these transactions, to the extent that they are business transactions, must be recorded in your accounting system.

Each transaction is made up of two sides of identical value. When you bought your pair of shoes, you received a pair of shoes that were worth exactly the same amount of cash that you paid for them. The service that you provided to your client was worth exactly the same amount that your client paid for that service. The amount of electricity that you consumed was worth exactly what you paid for it.

This is called the market economy and is the basis of the concept of market value.

But more important, from a bookkeeping perspective, was the economic flow. You paid cash out and received a tangible good in exchange. You provided a service and received cash in exchange. You received electricity for the money that you paid for it.

For every transaction there is an economic inflow that is exactly equal in dollar value to the economic outflow. Always remember that the economic flow inwards is a **debit** and the economic flow outwards is a **credit**.

Every single business transaction must be analysed to determine what was the inflow (debit) and what was the outflow (credit) and allocate a dollar value to each so that the dollar values of the inflow matches exactly the dollar values of the outflow.

For every transaction the total of all debits must equal the total of all credits.

An example of how this works is shown following.

We buy a pair of shoes. We receive the shoes (debit) in exchange for money paid (credit). The value of the shoes received is exactly the same as the value of the money paid. We provide a service and we receive the money in exchange. The value of our service provided (credit) is exactly the same as the value of the money received (debit). We pay our electricity account. We receive electricity (debit) and pay money in exchange (credit). This is shown in table 1.1 (overleaf).

Table 1.1: debits and credits

Debit	Credit
Shoes	Money
Money	Service
Electricity	Money

Account types

It's not enough to just consider what the economic inflow or outflow of each transaction was; you also have to determine the effect that that economic activity will have on your business structure.

Asset versus expense

Let's first examine the situation in which you pay cash out for something. The cash out is a credit but the debit you received was for what? If it is for something that has lasting value, such as a motor vehicle or office equipment, then we classify that debit as an *asset*. If the item purchased is consumed, it is then referred to as an *expense*.

An asset is something of lasting value whereas an expense is something that is consumed by the business within a short period of time. An example of different types of assets and expenses is shown in table 1.2.

It's easy to become confused about what is an asset and what is an expense. What if I was to purchase a fountain pen for $45? It would certainly last more than one accounting period but is it really an asset? Assets can also be defined as the 'substance' of the business.

Table 1.2: assets and expenses

Asset	Expense
Cash at Bank	Wages
Motor vehicles	Motor vehicle expenses
Office equipment	Electricity
Office furniture	Rates and taxes
Debtors (accounts receivable)	Interest paid
Land and buildings	Insurance
Furnishings	Purchases (COGS)

Minor items such as a fountain pen hardly meet that criteria and therefore we have a de minimis rule, which in this means that any whole item purchased for less than $300 is to be considered an expense. And since the Tax Office considers you to be a small business entity, as a concession it will allow you to 'expense' any complete asset that costs less than $1000. So the rule for small business is if it costs less than $1000, it is an expense; if it cost more than $1000 and is of lasting value, it is an asset.

Another murky area is your **inventory**, which can be considered both an asset and an expense. Your end-of-year stocktake establishes a balance that is considered to be an asset, whereas your day-to-day **purchases** are a special type of expense included in your **cost of sales** or, using the more traditional term, **cost of goods sold (COGS)**.

Liability versus income

Every **trading business** wishes to sell its goods—'get them out the door' is the catchcry of every salesperson. When you sell that pair of shoes, the money you receive is a debit to your bank account and the economic value of what you provide to your customer, the shoes, is classified as income and is a credit to sales.

On the other hand we may have received something on the promise that we will pay at a later date. A deferred payment or an obligation to pay is a liability.

As shown in table 1.3, income is the economic value of what we sold, whereas a liability is a legal obligation to pay.

Table 1.3: liability and income

Liability	Income
Bank overdraft	Sales
Loans	Commissions earned
Creditors (accounts payable)	Fees received

Owner's equity

It is very important that we recognise that from a bookkeeping perspective you and your business are two different entities. This is called the entity convention.

If you put money into your business bank account, you are giving that money to a completely separate entity, your business. Therefore, the business owes you that money. If the business owes money, that is a liability to the business.

Owner's equity is a general term used to define the money that is owed by the business to its owners. Owner's equity accounts are divided into three main types, with a fourth tax-specific type:

- *Capital.* The **Capital** account is a liability account that holds the value of the money and other assets, less any liabilities, that you transferred into the business when you created it. This is illustrated in example 1.1.

Example 1.1

I start a business by putting $10 000 in the bank. I transfer a motor vehicle worth $30 000 and the loan for the vehicle is worth $25 000. My Capital account would stand at $15 000.

Cash at Bank	$10 000	
Motor vehicle	$30 000	
Loan on vehicle		$25 000
Capital account		$15 000

My debits all equal my credits on the opening transaction.

- *Drawings*. Money that is drawn out of the business in the form of a payment, such as wages, is referred to as **drawings** and is accounted for separately from the capital. It is later offset against profits.
- *Retained earnings*. If the business makes a profit but does not distribute all of that profit to the owners, the balance is held in the Retained Earnings account.
- *Private use*. When the business assets, such as the office computer, will be shared with the family, especially when a small business is run from home, this is known as 'private use' in tax terms and must be accounted for separately from 'business use'. Using an equity account called 'Private Use' is my solution.

Note

In a partnership, each business owner will usually have their own complete set of equity accounts.

How much is my business worth?

Your business will have a set of asset accounts and some offsetting liability accounts. The difference between what the business owns and what the business owes is the balance owed to the owner of the business and should total the owner's equity accounts. This is called the balance sheet equation and is usually presented as assets minus liabilities equals owner's equity (A – L = E).

The building blocks of business transactions: categorising and summarising

The recording of business transactions is a process of analysing the transactions and placing ('**posting**' in accounting terms) the recognised component amounts into the appropriate categories and then summarising (end-of-period totals) the result. See example 1.2, which outlines the purchase of a motor vehicle and how it is categorised and summarised.

Example 1.2

Our first transaction is to buy a motor vehicle for $33 000 cash. A motor vehicle is an asset but the purchase price also contains an amount of GST. The cash came out of the bank account. So to record the vehicle purchase we will categorise the transaction into a credit amount to the bank account and split the debit amount between the motor vehicle account and the GST account, as is shown in the following tables:

Account name: Cash at Bank

Date	Particulars	Debit ($)	Credit ($)	Balance ($)
01/01/YY	Purchase Ford Falcon		33 000.00	(33 000.00)

Account name: Motor Vehicle (Ford Falcon)

Date	Particulars	Debit ($)	Credit ($)	Balance ($)
01/01/YY	Cash from Metro Cars	30 000.00		30 000.00

Account name: GST

Date	Particulars	Debit ($)	Credit ($)	Balance ($)
01/01/YY	Ford Falcon purchase	3000.00		3000.00

These categories are called general ledger accounts, often referred to as just 'the accounts'. The process of recording the amounts is called posting to the ledger.

The next set of transactions involves the costs of owning the vehicle, paying for insurance, registration, petrol and so on. Ignoring the cash at bank and GST amounts, the amounts expended are for a series of expenses. The question is to what account do we 'post' the amounts?

The answer to this question, like so many answers in accounting, is dependent on what information you wish to get out of your records. In other words, what are you going to use the accounting information for? In our case it is primarily for taxation purposes, both the GST via the BAS and for income tax. For this reason we only need to record the expense. One 'lump' sum for similar types of expenses at the end of the accounting period will suffice and therefore one account called Motor Vehicle Expenses will do.

However, from a management viewpoint we might wish to know just how much the new Ford Falcon is costing us compared with our existing fleet. As is shown in the following table, we would probably have one Motor Vehicle Expenses account for each separate motor vehicle, just as we would have a separate account for each motor vehicle asset.

Account name: Motor Vehicle Expenses (Ford Falcon)

Date	Particulars	Debit ($)	Credit ($)	Balance ($)
01/01/YY	Registration	653.28		653.28
01/01/YY	Insurance	1234.78		1888.06
10/01/YY	Fuel	56.87		1944.93
14/01/YY	Fuel	65.43		2009.36
21/01/YY	Fuel	38.93		2048.29
30/01/YY	Fuel	68.54		2116.83

Chart of accounts—the uniform system of accounts

If we're going to have a general ledger account for each type of asset, liability, income and expense item, our books of account are fast going to become very unwieldy.

Historically each account was given its own page in a book. The book was held together by two bolts so that it could be opened up and new pages added. Each account type was given its own section and each **ledger account** given a unique number within that section. So the assets had their own section, liabilities their own and so on. Each section had its own number and that number preceded the account number. As an example, if assets were recorded in the number 1 section and the motor vehicle account was recorded as number 250 within the assets section, then the full motor vehicle account number would be 1-250, or more often just 1250.

The index to this general ledger that contains this numbering system is called a **chart of accounts**. There is no accounting standard for a chart of accounts numbering system, so anything goes. This can make life a little difficult, especially in computerised systems, so a default standard has evolved. The history behind the common standard is that in 1926 the International Association of Hospitality Accountants set a standard within the hospitality industry called the Uniform System of Accounts. The first edition was published in 1926 by the Hotel Association of New York City; it has since become a standard across all business sectors.

The benefits of the Uniform System of Accounts is that it establishes standardised formats and account classifications to guide individuals in the preparation and presentation of financial statements.

In its most basic format the Uniform System of Accounts consists of a sequence of numbers for each classification type:

1	Assets	1000 to 1999
2	Liabilities	2000 to 2999
3	Owner's equity	3000 to 3999
4	Income	4000 to 4999
5	Cost of sales	5000 to 5999
6	Expenses	6000 to 6999
8	Other income	8000 to 8999
9	Other expenses	9000 to 9999

Note

We are *not* using the 7000 series here. I have chosen to do this to be consistent with MYOB but there is no reason why the 7000 series could not appear for 'Other income' and the 8000 series for 'Other expenses' leaving the 9000 series unused. See appendix A for details of MYOB's full accounting program.

In figure 1.1 you will see the basic layout of a balance sheet and an income statement.

Figure 1.1: balance sheet and income statement

	Balance sheet for the period ending ... / ... /		
1	**Assets**		
	Current assets		
	Noncurrent (fixed) assets		
	Intangible assets	________	
	Total assets	$	
2	**Liabilities**		
	Current liabilities		
	Noncurrent (long-term) liabilities	________	
	Total liabilities	$	
	Net Assets		$________
3	**Owners equity**		
	Capital contribution		
	Drawings		
	Retained earnings (from income statement)		________
	Total Equity		$________

Income statement for the period 1 July __ to 30 June __		
4 **Income**		
Total income		$
5 ***Less* cost of goods sold**		
Opening inventory		
Plus Purchases		
Freight inwards		
Customs duty	______	
Goods available for sale		
Less Closing inventory		______
Gross profit from trading		$
6 ***Less* expenses**		
Marketing		
Administrative		
Financial		______
Net profit from trading		$
7 ***Plus* other income**		
8 ***Less* other expenses**		______
Net profit (transferred to retained earnings)		$______

We will use the balance sheet and income statement from figure 1.1. to create a chart of accounts for our own use, as shown in table 1.4.

Table 1.4: the standard chart of accounts

1000 to 1999	Assets
1100	Cash at Bank
1190	Inventory as at 01/07/20XX

Table 1.4 *(cont'd)*: the standard chart of accounts

1200	Accounts receivable (debtors or trade receivables)
1550	Motor vehicles
1555	Accumulated depreciation (motor vehicles)
1570	Office furniture and equipment
1575	Accumulated depreciation (office equipment)
2000 to 2999	**Liabilities**
2150	Loan account
2200	Accounts payable (creditors or trade payables)
3000 to 3999	**Owner's equity**
3110	R Brown capital
3220	R Brown drawings
3310	Private use
3400	Retained earnings
4000 to 4999	**Income (from trading activities)**
4100	Sales
4110	Sales returns (accrual accounting only)
4120	Allowances given (accrual accounting only)
5000 to 5999	**Cost of sales**
5100	Opening inventory (for use by your accountant)
5200	Purchases
5210	Freight outwards
5220	Freight inwards
5300	Closing inventory (for use by your accountant)
6000 to 6999	**Expenses (usually expressed in alphabetical order and sometimes subdivided)**
6100	Advertising
6130	Depreciation expense (for use by your accountant)

6150	Electricity and power
6170	Interest paid
6190	Rent (commercial rent includes GST)
8000 to 8999	**Other income (income not from trading activities)**
8100	Interest received
8200	Profit on sale of assets
9000 to 9999	**Other expenses (expenses not incurred in trading)**
9200	Loss on sale of assets
9500	Income tax expense

You will notice from the previous entries that items are initially allocated numbers at least 10 digits apart. This is to allow new accounts to be created in the correct sequence. As an example, expenses consists of the following:

6100	Advertising
6130	Depreciation expense
6150	Electricity and power
6170	Interest paid
6190	Rent

If we were required to include bank charges in the these entries, we could insert it as 6120 without altering the initial codes, as you can see following:

6100	Advertising
6120	Bank charges
6130	Depreciation expense
6150	Electricity and power
6170	Interest paid
6190	Rent

These classifications are very similar to the most common 'off the shelf' computerised accounting packages used in small business. In such packages the chart of accounts also includes embedded headings to facilitate automated reporting. The chart of accounts in either manual or computerised systems controls the whole process of recording accounting data from the very first data entry to the final report.

Chart of accounts exercise

Using your own business or one that you are familiar with, we are going to create a chart of accounts that will suit your business. We will use the standard model:

1	Assets	1000 to 1999
2	Liabilities	2000 to 2999
3	Owner's equity (your ownership interest in the business)	3000 to 3999
4	Income	4000 to 4999
5	Cost of sales (often referred to as cost of goods sold, COGS)	5000 to 5999
6	Expenses	6000 to 6999
8	Other income	8000 to 8999
9	Other expenses	9000 to 9999

Note

Item 7 does not exist as we are using the MYOB structure in this example.

1 Assets

An asset is something that is of lasting value to the business and has an initial cost in excess of $1000 (a small business concession), such as a motor vehicle. There are two forms of assets, those that you expect to be converted into cash within the next 12 months and those of a more enduring nature.

A **current asset** is the first type of asset and your **cash at bank** account is the most common example. Other assets expected to be converted into cash within the next 12 months are your opening inventory amount and debtors (also called **trade debtors** or **trade receivables**); however, as a cash-based system we don't usually record our debtors in the general ledger but keep it within a separate debtors ledger.

1000	Current assets	*(Heading)*
1100	Cash at Bank	
1200	Inventory as of 1 July	

In this list you will also notice a classification called 'Heading'. This account isn't to be used to accumulate expenditure but rather it is to be used as a reporting tool. It is unusual (and unnecessary) to include 'Heading' accounts in a manual chart of accounts but since they are usually required for computerised systems, they have been included here.

A **noncurrent asset** is an asset that is of a more enduring nature. These assets, with the exception of land, are usually depreciated over their effective life and therefore will have an accumulated depreciation account attached to them, as the following entries show:

1500	Noncurrent (fixed) assets	*(Heading)*
1520	Land	
1550	Factory unit	

1555	Accumulated depreciation factory unit
1610	Ford panel van
1615	Accumulated depreciation Ford panel van
1620	Holden sedan
1625	Accumulated depreciation Holden sedan
1720	Office equipment
1725	Accumulated depreciation office equipment

Note

A special type of noncurrent asset is called an intangible asset. These are assets that have no physical form, although they are still of future value to the business. The most common types of intangible assets are trademarks and patents. It is unusual for a small business to hold intangible assets, with the exception of incorporation expenses for businesses running as registered private companies (Pty Ltd).

2 Liabilities

A liability is something that we owe to another entity, a future expense. The most common example is our business loans. As with assets, liabilities are divided into **current liabilities**, which must be satisfied within the next 12 months such as our credit card debt, and **noncurrent liabilities**, which can be satisfied in the longer term, such as a mortgage.

Current liabilities are any expenses that are 'recognised' and due to be paid within the next 12 months. To be recognised, the amount must be a current 'legal' liability and not just a future expectation. One of the most important current liability accounts is the GST account, which accumulates the 'net' amount that you owe to the Tax Office.

2000	Current liabilities *(Heading)*
2100	Visa card balance
2150	Mortgage repayments for next 12 months
2190	GST
2500	Noncurrent (long-term) liabilities *(Heading)*
2550	Mortgage over factory unit

Note

Some systems run two GST accounts, one for amounts paid and one for amounts collected. They are then netted off at the end of the financial quarter to obtain the amount payable. I do not see the need for two accounts and prefer to run the one account that shows the daily position in regard to my GST liability.

3 Owner's equity

Let's use an example to explain the term equity. You buy a house for \$500 000 and take out a mortgage for \$300 000. Your equity in the house is said to be \$200 000, which is the part of the house that is really yours as distinct from the part owned by the bank. Therefore, your house is owned by your bank and you.

House = Bank + Equity

It is the same for a business. The business assets have been 'funded' partly through borrowings, your liabilities, and partly through your own contributions, your equity. It can be expressed as either A – L = E or A = L + E.

This relationship is called the balance sheet equation and is used by your accountant when preparing your end-of-year reports.

Equity accounts are usually divided into a set of four separate accounts, one set for each 'owner'.

3000	Equity (proprietorship)	*(Heading)*
3200	Capital (J Bloggs)	
3300	Drawings (J Bloggs)	
3400	Private use (J Bloggs)	
3500	Retained earnings (J Bloggs)	

Of course, in a sole proprietor situation you will have only one 'set' but in a partnership you will have one set for each partner. Trusts and companies have a slightly different structure for their equity accounts but they work principally the same.

Note

The 'private use' account is not usually included but it is my suggested method of accounting for the private use of business assets by the owners. See day 6 for further details on private use.

4 Revenue or income

Revenue or income accounts report the amounts that we receive from our business activities. They could be classified as sales if we are a trading organisation or fees if we are a service industry, and can be broken up into as many classifications as we require. When making these classifications the question we must ask ourselves is what do we need to know at the end of the year about the source of our business revenue.

4000	Revenue (income) *(Heading)*
4100	Fees earned from lawn mowing
4200	Fees earned from landscaping
4300	Sales of landscaping materials
4900	Other business income

Note

Revenue accounts hold business income only. Other forms of income, such as interest received from bank accounts or profits made from the sale of assets, are accounted for under 'Other business income'.

5 Cost of sales (or COGS)

For trading enterprises, the gross profit is the difference between your purchase price and the selling price of your merchandise. When you buy **stock** (inventory) it is applied to a Purchases account. The inventory accounts are never altered as a result of your trading activity. Inventory is only ever accounted for as a result of your annual stocktake.

Therefore, for a service industry you will not have any accounts under cost of sales. For a trading enterprise you will have purchases, plus anything that is added to your cost of sales, such as transport and insurance inwards and clearance expenses. Any costs **incurred** in getting the goods to your back door are your cost of sales.

However, some of your purchases will be carried over to the following financial year and your initial sales were probably from last year's inventory that was carried over. Therefore the true cost of sales is the cost of your purchases modified by your movement in inventory. This calculation is done by your accountant at the end of the financial year. We simply include the opening and closing inventory accounts for your accountant's end-of-year calculations.

5000	Cost of sales *(Heading)*
5100	Opening inventory
5200	Purchases
5220	Transport inwards
5230	Insurance inwards
5240	Clearance expenses
5400	Closing inventory

Note

Inventory accounts are for your accountant's end-of-year calculations and are not to be used in day-to-day processing. All purchases of inventory are posted to the purchases account and all sales of inventory to a sales account.

6 Expenses

The expenses listed in this section include your normal day-to-day running costs of the business, such as power, petrol, stationery and wages. However, these are 'normal' business expenses. Any abnormal or extraordinary expenses are accounted for under 'other expenses'. This would include items such as loss on sale of assets, which is any residue that you can claim as a business expense when it comes time to dispose of a business asset.

When accounting for motor vehicle expenses it's a good idea to group them according to the specific motor vehicle that they apply to, which will help your accountant at the end of the financial year. Also, any item that has both a private and a business component should be accounted for separately, such as a home-office telephone account.

As the following example shows, the expenses for a small business are traditionally listed alphabetically:

6000	Expenses *(Heading)*
6100	Advertising
6130	Depreciation expense (for use by your accountant)
6150	Electricity and power
6160	Interest paid
6170	Internet
6180	Insurance
6210	Motor vehicle expenses (Ford panel van)
6220	Motor vehicle expenses (Holden sedan)
6310	Rent (commercial rent includes GST)
6320	Telephone
6610	Wages and salaries paid
6615	Wages overtime
6620	Wages—PAYG
6630	Wages—superannuation
6635	Wages—workers compensation insurance

8 Other income

The expenses in this section and the following section, 'other expenses', are used to hold amounts of an unusual or infrequent nature, or amounts incurred or received that are outside your normal course of trading activities. Holding these amounts separate from your normal trading income and expenses will allow you to determine your true profit from your trading activities.

Income not in the normal course of trading:

8000 Other income (*Heading*)

8100 Interest received

8200 Profit on disposal of assets

9 Other expenses

As just described under 'other income', this account is used to hold abnormal or extraordinary expenses.

9000 Other expenses (*Heading*)

9200 Loss on disposal of assets

9300 Income tax expense

Exercise 1.1

Create a chart of accounts for your particular business, or for a business that you would like to begin. Please include all of the items that we have discussed in this section as we will be using them in our future exercises.

Computerised accounting: getting started

Computers can be considered either idiots with a fantastic memory or incredibly helpful tools provided they are approached in the most sensible way. With this in mind you must tell a computerised accounting program every minute detail of your business and its transactions in order for your accounting program to come to the correct conclusions.

When you open any accounting program for the first time it will ask you for your business details, such as name, address and ABN, as well as your financial details, such as the financial year that you are operating in, the last month of the financial year and so on. In multicompany programs, such as MYOB, your name is often used as the name of the company file.

After recording this initial information the next step in any accounting system, whether manual or computerised, is to set up your chart of accounts. Computerised accounting programs will usually provide you with an example set, often tailored towards particular business types that you then have to adapt for your own purposes.

In MYOB the classifications are 1 to 9; however, as the following example shows, it uses a slightly different format:

1–1000 to 1–9999 for assets
2–1000 to 2–9999 for liabilities
3–1000 to 3–9999 for equity
4–1000 to 4–9999 for income
5–1000 to 5–9999 for cost of sales
6–1000 to 6–9999 for expenses
8–1000 to 8–9999 for other income
9–1000 to 9–9999 for other expenses

This is exactly consistent with our approach; however, I find the 1000-, 2000-, 3000-type format easier in manual bookkeeping rather than the 1–1000-, 2–1000-, 3–1000-style format that is more suited to computerised accounting.

The setting up of a chart of accounts is crucial for any computerised accounting system and it is very hard to alter at a later date. Time spent on getting this part of your system correct from the outset is well worth the effort.

Your chart of accounts will govern all aspects of your bookkeeping and flows into the accounting, reporting and budgeting processes. For this reason it's not a good idea to blindly accept the systems-recommended accounts but rather to select ones closest to your own business situation and then modify them to suit your own particular needs.

Please refer to appendix A for details of where to download training versions of full computerised accounting programs. You might like to try exercise 1.1 again in a computer 'training' environment. Any accounting program's training version will be suitable, but in this book I use MYOB's examples as it is the most common accounting program used for small businesses in Australia, even though it's not necessarily the easiest program to use.

In MYOB, like most accounting programs, you will be first asked to create a new company and to supply all of the company's details. After this you can select a 'default' chart of accounts. MYOB offers many varieties, but just choose the one that is the closest fit for your needs. Now select the 'Command Centre'.

You can now edit your selected default chart of accounts through the Command Centre's Accounts page by selecting the 'Accounts List' menu item. From here you can add, edit or delete any of the accounts until your chart of accounts matches your exact requirements. The screenshot in figure 1.2 shows a default chart of accounts.

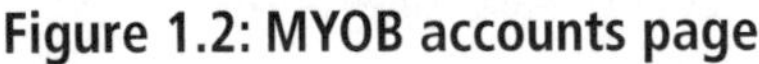

Figure 1.2: MYOB accounts page

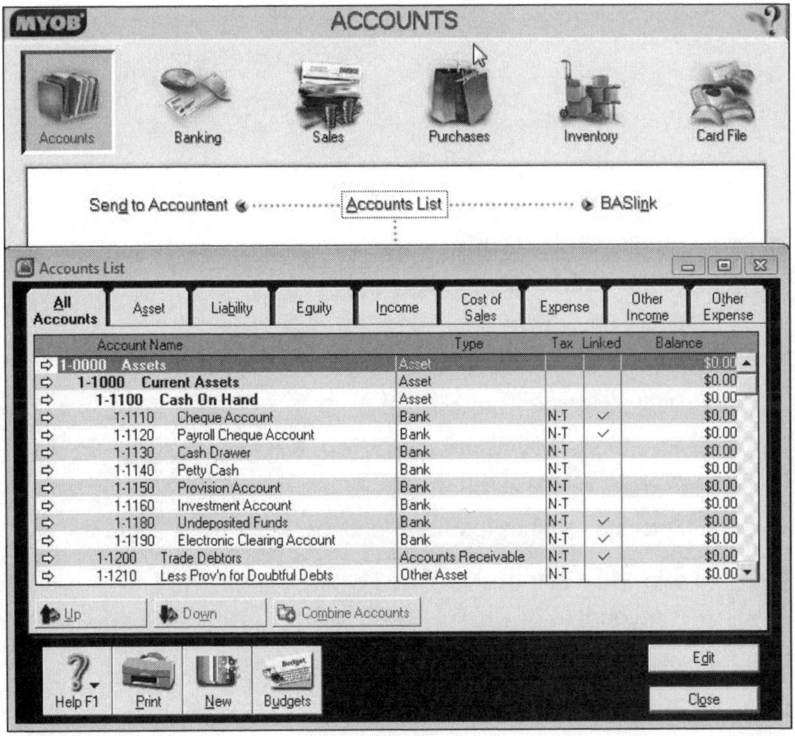

MYOB ACCOUNTS

Accounts | Banking | Sales | Purchases | Inventory | Card File

Send to Accountant · Accounts List · BASlink

Accounts List

All Accounts | Asset | Liability | Equity | Income | Cost of Sales | Expense | Other Income | Other Expense

	Account Name	Type	Tax	Linked	Balance
⇨	**1-0000 Assets**	Asset			$0.00
⇨	**1-1000 Current Assets**	Asset			$0.00
⇨	**1-1100 Cash On Hand**	Asset			$0.00
⇨	1-1110 Cheque Account	Bank	N-T	✓	$0.00
⇨	1-1120 Payroll Cheque Account	Bank	N-T	✓	$0.00
⇨	1-1130 Cash Drawer	Bank	N-T		$0.00
⇨	1-1140 Petty Cash	Bank	N-T		$0.00
⇨	1-1150 Provision Account	Bank	N-T		$0.00
⇨	1-1160 Investment Account	Bank	N-T		$0.00
⇨	1-1180 Undeposited Funds	Bank	N-T	✓	$0.00
⇨	1-1190 Electronic Clearing Account	Bank	N-T	✓	$0.00
⇨	1-1200 Trade Debtors	Accounts Receivable	N-T	✓	$0.00
⇨	1-1210 Less Prov'n for Doubtful Debts	Other Asset	N-T		$0.00

Up | Down | Combine Accounts

Help F1 | Print | New | Budgets | Edit | Close

When you create a new account you will need to give it a number and name but you also need to apply a GST code under 'details'. This is the default GST code that will drive the BAS report. See day 6 for a complete discussion on GST codes and the BAS.

Revision exercise for day 1

1 In the following list indicate which should be classified as an asset, liability, equity, income, cost of sales or expense:

Sales
Wages
Cash at Bank
Loan account
Drawings
Purchases
Motor vehicle at cost
Motor vehicle expenses
Office equipment
Repairs and maintenance
Debtors (accounts receivable)
Creditors (accounts payable)
Owner's capital account
Retained earnings (profits of prior periods)

2 If I sold you a pair of shoes, do I debit or credit the sales account?

3 If I paid a Western Power bill, do I debit or credit the electricity account?

4 Please fill in the headings in the following general ledger account:

Account name: Motor Vehicle Expenses (Ford Falcon)

01/01/YY	Registration	653.28		653.28
01/01/YY	Insurance	1234.78		1888.06

Day 2

Analysing and recording transactions

Key terms and concepts

- *Journal:* where we first enter a transaction; it is then transferred to the general ledger.
- *Posting:* the term used when we transfer an amount from the journal to the general ledger.
- *General ledger account:* more commonly known as 'ledger account', holds the records of the transactions that relate to the one chart of account item.
- A single general ledger account holds the details of one classification item as per the chart of accounts. For example, the Electricity account holds all of the details of the payments made for your business's electricity usage.
- General ledger accounts hold the details of the entire year's transactions. They are closed off at the end of each financial year and a new account is opened at the beginning of the following financial year.

Bookkeeping is a process of classifying, recording, summarising and proving business transactions. We learnt on day 1 that business transactions can be categorised into assets, liabilities, equity, income, cost of sales and expense. The method we use to classify our business data is based upon a chart of accounts. The structure of a business's chart of accounts is 'theoretically' entirely of that businesses's own making, but as computerised accounting packages are standardised on a set structure, for the purposes of this book we have adopted that structure as our own.

Our next step is to record our transactions.

Transaction analysis

In this section we will look at some common transactions and determine the debit and credit amounts of each transaction and the correct classification of those amounts according to our chart of accounts classifications. At this stage we will ignore the GST.

We have already done this once when looking at the owner's capital accounts in day 1. Now let's revisit this in example 2.1 to refresh our memory about debits and credits.

Example 2.1

I start a business by putting $10 000 in the bank. I transfer a motor vehicle worth $30 000, with a loan for the vehicle worth $25 000. My capital account stands at $15 000.

Account description	Debit ($)	Credit ($)
Cash at Bank	10 000	
Motor vehicle	30 000	
Loan account		25 000
Capital		15 000

What is missing from this example are the dates that these transactions took place. All business transactions occur on a particular date and as there is usually more than one transaction taking place in any period, the dates must be recorded to avoid confusion. See below for the correct way to record these transactions.

02/01/YY Received fee of $850.

03/01/YY Paid telephone account of $156.98.

15/01/YY Paid electricity account of $167.88.

26/01/YY Paid wages of $1267.89.

30/01/YY Bought a computer for cash costing $1545.90.

Date	Account description	Debit ($)	Credit ($)
02/01/YY	Cash at Bank	850.00	
	Fees		850.00
03/01/YY	Telephone	156.98	
	Cash at Bank		156.98
15/01/YY	Electricity	167.88	
	Cash at Bank		167.88
26/01/YY	Wages	1267.89	
	Cash at Bank		1267.89
30/01/YY	Office equipment	1545.90	
	Cash at Bank		1545.90

Put your learnings to the test with exercise 2.1 (overleaf).

Exercise 2.1

Analyse the following transactions. Note that you enter the transaction on the date it occurred, not the date you are making the entry, which could be some time later.

02/02/YY	Made a cash sale of $345.98.
03/02/YY	Paid telephone account of $267.89.
15/02/YY	Purchased inventory for cash costing $234.12.
26/02/YY	Paid myself $897.56.
30/02/YY	Bought an office desk for cash costing $645.

Please use a form drawn up as follows. They can also be downloaded from my website <www.tpabusiness.com.au>.

Date	Account description	Debit ($)	Credit ($)

There are a few everyday transactions that need a little explanation. If I sell something for cash, I debit the Cash at Bank account and credit the Sales account; however, if I sell something on credit, I credit Sales and debit the **Debtors account** (**Accounts Receivable**).

If I purchase inventory for resale, I debit the Purchases account and credit the Cash at Bank account. If I purchase inventory on credit, I debit Purchases and credit the **Creditors account** (**Accounts Payable**).

If I purchase an asset on credit terms, such as a motor vehicle, I will debit the assets account Motor Vehicles with the value of the motor vehicle purchased and credit the liability account that I have created in the name of the vendor with the amount owing. This account is called a **sundry creditors** account and is not to be confused with the 'Creditors' account, which is solely for the **credit purchase** of inventory for resale.

In exercise 2.2 we will examine a few common credit transactions.

Exercise 2.2

Analyse the following details and transfer them to a form with the following headings.

04/02/YY Made a credit sale of $345.98.

16/02/YY Purchased inventory on credit for $234.12.

27/02/YY Bought an office desk from MyOffice on credit for $645.

Date	Account description	Debit ($)	Credit ($)

The only difference between a **general journal** as shown following and the previous 'transaction analysis' is that the general journal has a column for a folio reference number and an explanation provided after each entry. The folio is used as a cross-reference when posting to the general ledger accounts. The format of a general journal is as shown in table 2.1 (overleaf).

Table 2.1: sample general journal format

Company name: **GJ1**

Date	Particulars	Debit ($)	Credit ($)	Balance ($)

A general journal can contain as many rows as required. Often these accounting forms are allocated a page to themselves.

The format of a general ledger account (one for each chart of account item) is shown in table 2.2.

Table 2.2: sample general ledger account

Account name: **Folio number:**

Date	Details	Folio	Debit ($)	Credit ($)	Balance ($)

It should be noted that this general ledger account form is called a 'running balance account' as distinct from a '**T account**', which is also often used in manual bookkeeping. I have chosen to use the running balance style because this is the type of form you will find in computerised accounting packages.

Posting to the ledger

The next step to learn is how to post to the general ledger. Let's revisit exercise 2.1 and complete the example using the general journal format, as shown in table 2.3.

Table 2.3: completed general journal example

Company name: My Company & Sons

Date	Particulars	Folio	Debit ($)	Credit ($)
02/02/YY	Cash at Bank	1100	345.98	
	Cash sales	4100		345.98
	Being: Cash sale till receipts for the day			
03/02/YY	Telephone	6200	267.89	
	Cash at Bank	1100		267.89
	Being: Telecom bill for the month			
15/02/YY	Purchases	5100	234.12	
	Cash at Bank	1100		234.12
	Being: Cash purchase for the month			
26/02/YY	Drawings	3120	897.56	
	Cash at Bank	1100		897.56
	Being: Owner's monthly drawings			
30/02/YY	Office furniture	1400	645.00	
	Cash at Bank	1100		645.00
	Being: Pam's new desk			

In table 2.4 (overleaf) we will 'post' the items to the general ledger accounts. Although the example in table 2.3 already has the folio numbers entered, it is in fact at this point that those numbers are entered, one at a time as each amount is posted to its own individual account. Please note, there is only one account per chart of account item. For example, there is only one Cash at Bank account and one Sales account.

Table 2.4: posting items to general ledger accounts

Account name: Cash at Bank **Folio number: 1100**

Date	Details	Folio	Debit ($)	Credit ($)	Balance ($)
2/2/YY	Cash sales	GJ1	345.98		345.98
3/2/YY	Telephone	GJ1		267.89	78.09
15/2/YY	Purchases	GJ1		234.12	(156.03)
26/2/YY	Drawings	GJ1		897.56	(1053.59)
30/2/YY	Office furniture	GJ1		645.00	(1698.59)

As is shown in table 2.4, the account name is in accord with your chart of accounts name and the folio number is likewise in accord with your chart of accounts number. The first number of the folio number indicates the chart of accounts type; in this case the account is an asset (1 asset, 2 liability, 3 equity, 4 income, 5 cost of sales, 6 expenses).

As table 2.5 shows, the running balance is adjusted every time an item is added to the account. If the amount is shown in parentheses, it is a credit balance. Note again that the date of postings in the general ledger from the general journal is the date of the transaction, not the date it was posted.

Table 2.5: running balances

Account name: Cash Sales **Folio number: 4100**

Date	Details	Folio	Debit ($)	Credit ($)	Balance ($)
2/2/YY	Daily till receipt	GJ1		345.98	(345.98)

Account name: Telephone **Folio number: 6200**

Date	Details	Folio	Debit ($)	Credit ($)	Balance ($)
3/2/YY	Telecom account #12345	GJ1	267.89		267.89

Let's complete exercise 2.3 to cement our knowledge.

Exercise 2.3

Following the format we have just used and using the transactions outlined in exercise 2.1, complete the remaining accounts in the forms drawn up as shown.

Account name: Purchases **Folio number: 5100**

Date	Details	Folio	Debit ($)	Credit ($)	Balance ($)

Account name: Drawings **Folio number: 3120**

Date	Details	Folio	Debit ($)	Credit ($)	Balance ($)

Account name: Office Furniture **Folio number: 1400**

Date	Details	Folio	Debit ($)	Credit ($)	Balance ($)

Having completed posting to the general ledger for the *month*, we now have to prove that our posting was correct. We do this by checking that the sum of all of our debit balances equals the sum of our credit balances. The form we use to do this is called a trial balance, as shown in table 2.6.

Table 2.6: blank trial balance form

Trial Balance

Company Name .... **as at** .... / .... / ....

Account #	Account name	Debit ($)	Credit ($)
	TOTALS		

Using the transactions we have analysed from exercise 2.1, table 2.7 shows how our trial balance will look. Note that all of the entries in the trial balance are in chart of accounts number order.

Table 2.7: completed trial balance form

Trial Balance

Company Name .... **as at** .... / .... / ....

Account #	Account name	Debit ($)	Credit ($)
1100	Cash at Bank		1698.59
1400	Office Furniture	645.00	
3120	Drawings	897.56	
4100	Cash Sales		345.98
5100	Purchases	234.12	
6200	Telephone	267.89	
	TOTALS	2044.57	2044.57

(Debits must equal the credits)

Let's practise our skills with exercise 2.4.

Exercise 2.4

Let's revisit exercise 2.2, by using the general journal, posting our transactions to the general ledger and proving our postings via the trial balance. Following are our original transactions:

04/02/YY	Made a **credit sale** of $345.98.
16/02/YY	Purchased inventory on credit for $234.12.
27/02/YY	Bought an office desk from MyOffice on credit for $645.

Please use a form drawn up as shown below. They can also be downloaded from my website <www.tpabusiness.com.au>.

Company name: **GJ1**

Date	Particulars	Folio	Debit ($)	Credit ($)

Now post all of your journal entries to the general ledger, as shown in the following tables:

Account name: **Folio number:**

Date	Details	Folio	Debit ($)	Credit ($)	Balance ($)

Account name: **Folio number:**

Date	Details	Folio	Debit ($)	Credit ($)	Balance ($)

Exercise 2.4 *(cont'd)*

Account name: **Folio number:**

Date	Details	Folio	Debit ($)	Credit ($)	Balance ($)

Account name: **Folio number:**

Date	Details	Folio	Debit ($)	Credit ($)	Balance ($)

Account name: **Folio number:**

Date	Details	Folio	Debit ($)	Credit ($)	Balance ($)

Account name: **Folio number:**

Date	Details	Folio	Debit ($)	Credit ($)	Balance ($)

And now finally transfer all of the balances to the trial balance as shown in the following table.

Trial Balance

Company name: .... **as at** .... / .... / ....

Account #	Account name	Debit ($)	Credit ($)
	TOTALS		

What an exercise! Fortunately there is an easier way to record this information—in 'cash journals', which are fully discussed in day 3.

Computerised accounting

In computerised accounting programs, such as MYOB, you enter journal entries in exactly the same way as you do for a manual system; however, the posting to the general ledger accounts and the trial balance are automated processes undertaken as you enter the original data into the journal. The screenshot in figure 2.1 shows the MYOB general journal input screen, which is almost identical with our own manual general journal form.

Figure 2.1: MYOB record journal entry

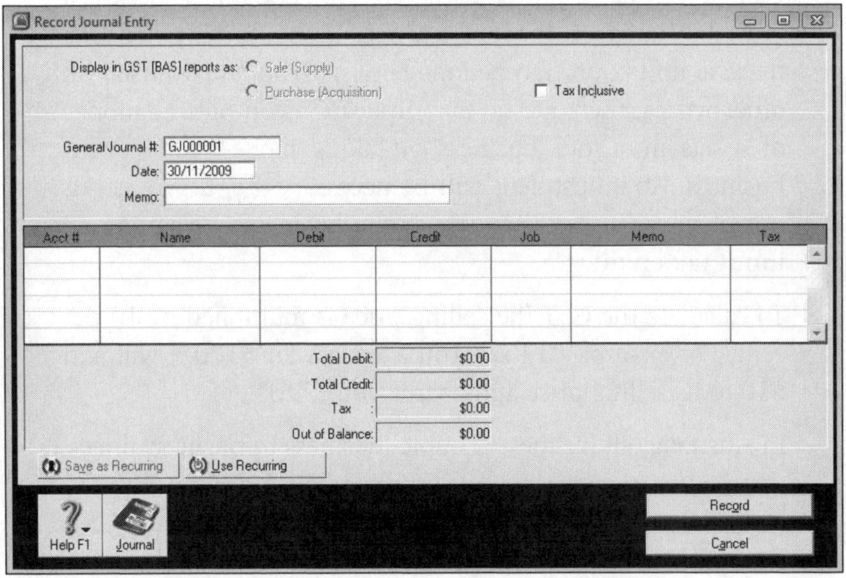

The GST

Before we delve further into bookkeeping, we must address the issue of goods and services tax (GST). Since this is not a book about taxation, but rather bookkeeping, we will explain how to account for the GST without going into the intricacies of the tax itself.

The GST is Australia's implementation of the value added tax (VAT) that has been slowly adopted by most OECD countries over the last 50 years. The USA is the only 'advanced' economy not to have adopted the GST (or VAT) in lieu of sales tax.

In Australia there is only one rate of GST, and that is 10 per cent. Some goods and services are exempt from the tax, but most goods and services are subject to the tax. Very few business transactions are not subject to the GST. Government charges and financial 'supplies', such as interest, do not include GST. If GST is included in the cost of goods or a service, it must be stated on the 'tax' invoice. It should be noted that there is no tax on transactions between you and yourself; in other words, there are no tax implications on putting money or assets into your business or taking money out of your business. An adjustment will be necessary if you take goods out of your business for which the business is claiming an **input tax credit**.

To calculate the GST the selling price is multiplied by 10 per cent. For example, if I sell you a widget for $100, I will add $10 to its selling price and charge you $110.

In Australia, all businesses quote 'business to business prices' that do not include the GST; however, when dealing with the final **consumer**, the price quoted must be inclusive of GST. For this reason, when we go shopping for a pair of shoes the price tag quoted is the price we pay. This is not the case in other countries.

If we purchase an item that includes the GST, to calculate the amount of GST included we divide the purchase price by 11. For example, if we buy a widget for $110, we divide

$110 by $11 and we discover that $10 is the amount of GST included.

GST is applied to the final sales price irrespective of how that price is calculated. For example, if you get a mates' rates discount that is not available to anyone else, the GST is calculated on your reduced cost, not the original selling price to the wider community:

Catalogue price	$1000.00
Special cost to hurry delivery	$50.00
Mates' rate discount 20%	–$210.00
Gold plating extra	$25.00
Cost price	$865.00
GST	$86.50
Final price inclusive of GST	$951.50

If you 'forget' to include the GST in your selling price, you wear it. By law, the amount of GST included in the selling price is deemed to be 1/11 of the sale value. There's no getting out of it.

If your business is expected to have an annual turnover in excess of $75 000, you must register for the GST. Most small businesses will register for the GST and pay the GST on a quarterly basis using a form sent out quarterly by the Tax Office called a Business Activity Statement (BAS). If you keep your records in accordance with the procedure outlined in this book, you should have no problems completing your quarterly BAS form.

A word of caution, however. You can only claim the tax credits on purchases in excess of $80 that are accompanied by a **tax invoice**, which is an invoice that is headed 'tax invoice' and indicates the supplier's ABN and all of the necessary information needed for you to calculate your GST input tax credit. There are actually different requirements for invoices under $1000 and for those over $1000 but for simplicity most businesses ignore this and make sure that all of their invoices comply with the more stringent requirements. Following are the requirements that each invoice issued by your business must include:

1. The words 'tax invoice' stated prominently.
2. Your business name.
3. Your business ABN.
4. The date the tax invoice was issued.
5. The buyer's name.
6. The buyer's address and/or ABN.
7. A brief description of the items sold.
8. For each description, the quantity of the goods or the extent of services sold.
9. The GST-inclusive price of the taxable sale.
10. The GST amount—this can be shown separately or, if the GST to be paid is exactly one-eleventh of the total price, as a statement such as 'Total price includes GST'.

Accounting for the GST

In your chart of accounts you will have a liability account called GST. Let us assume that it is has been allocated a chart of accounts number of 2900. The fact that it holds a '2' means that it's a liability account. This account will hold the amount of GST that we must pay the Tax Office.

Note

Most accounting system use two GST accounts—one for GST paid and one for the GST received. At the end of each GST period (quarterly) you must offset one against the other to calculate the GST owing. I find this a cumbersome exercise and completely unnecessary. For the purposes of this book we will use one GST account.

The amounts that you include in your accounting records will be 'stripped' of their GST component. The GST amount will be added to or subtracted from the GST account balance. Therefore all amounts in your accounting records will exclude the GST.

When you make a purchase that contains a GST amount, the transaction is broken into the amount of goods or services purchased and the GST. This is illustrated in example 2.2.

Example 2.2

I purchase 100 widgets at $123 each for cash. As this is a business transaction I will expect to pay $12 300 plus $1230 GST, a total price of $13 530. This will be entered into my journal as Purchases indicating $12 300 of inventory and $1230 of GST with a corresponding credit to my bank account of the total amount paid of $13 530.

Date	Particulars	Folio	Debit ($)	Credit ($)
04/02/YY	Purchases	5100	12 300.00	
	GST	2900	1230.00	
	Cash at Bank	1100		13 530.00
	Being: Purchase of inventory for cash			

Note

Even though the GST is a liability account it is being debited with an amount. The GST account is 'usually' in credit (that is, we owe money to the Tax Office); however, it occasionally can go into debit (we are owed a refund). This does not alter its status as a liability account.

If we were to sell the same goods on credit, the journal entry would appear as shown in table 2.8.

Table 2.8: sale on credit

Date	Particulars	Folio	Debit ($)	Credit ($)
05/02/YY	Debtors (accounts receivable)	1500	13 530.00	
	Sales	4100		12 300.00
	GST	2900		1230.00
	Being: Sale on credit			

However, when the account is settled we do not account for the GST a second time, as shown in table 2.9. The settlement of an account is not the supply of a good or service, as that occurred in the original transaction.

Table 2.9: settlement of the account

Date	Particulars	Folio	Debit ($)	Credit ($)
10/02/YY	Cash at Bank	1100	13 530.00	
	Debtors (accounts receivable)	1500		13 530.00
	Being: Settlement of the account			

You will also notice that the amount of GST debited on purchase of the inventory (see example 2.2) is exactly the same as the amount of GST credited on its sale (see table 2.8). One offsets the other, which means that we are not left with a GST liability to pay. This occurred because we sold the goods for exactly the same amount that we bought them for, which is most unusual in business and would quickly lead to bankruptcy.

Let us assume that we make a 50 per cent mark-up. As shown in table 2.10, the goods would now be sold for $18 450 plus $1845 GST.

Table 2.10: sale on credit with 50 per cent mark-up

Date	Particulars	Folio	Debit ($)	Credit ($)
05/02/YY	Debtors (accounts receivable)	1500	20 295.00	
	Sales	4100		18 450.00
	GST	2900		1845.00
	Being: Sale on credit with 50% mark-up			

To summarise, we bought the goods for $12 300 (plus GST) for which we paid $13 530. We then sold them for $18 450 (plus GST) and therefore made a profit of $6150 ($18 450 minus $12 300). The GST does not play any part in the profit calculations. Table 2.11 reveals how our GST account would look.

Table 2.11: GST account

Account name: GST **Folio number: 2900**

Date	Details	Folio	Debit ($)	Credit ($)	Balance ($)
4/02/YY	Purchase	GJ1	1230.00		1230.00
5/02/YY	Sales	GJ1		1845.00	(615.00)

We now owe the Tax Office $615 in GST paid on our 'profit margin'. This is how the GST (VAT) works. It taxes the profit margin at every stage of the supply chain, not just at the end transaction as the sales tax does. This makes the GST far more difficult to evade.

Let's complete exercise 2.5 to put our newfound know-ledge of GST to the test.

Exercise 2.5

Using the following table consider whether the GST is included in the cost price/selling price of the following items for a small business (sole proprietorship or family partnership). If the answer is no, analyse the determining factors why not.

	Yes	No	Why; exempt, input taxed
Domestic rent			
Commercial rent			

	Yes	No	Why; exempt, input taxed
Wages			
Drawings			
Electricity			
Paid creditor $1200			
Council rates			
Received $1500 from J Bloggs on account			
Motor vehicle purchase			
Bank charges/Interest			
Wages on-costs Superannuation			
Workers Comp Insurance			
PAYG			
Capital contribution by owner			
Motor vehicle contributed by owner			
Inventory used by owners			
Building insurance			
Milk for staff coffee			
Office furniture			
Computer software			
Accountant's fees			

Computerised accounting and the GST

In most computerised accounting programs, the GST component of the purchase or sale is calculated automatically and the correct net amounts posted. However, in order for this to happen the correct GST amount has to be recorded in the program set-up files. Each computerised accounting package has a different method of doing this.

In most accounting programs the GST code and sometimes the BAS code is allocated to the account number in the chart of accounts as a default. Therefore, whenever you select an account you are also selecting a GST treatment and a BAS reporting method. What this means is that each account should contain amounts that have an identical GST and BAS treatment. For example, if you purchase inventory that is both subject to the GST and **GST free**, then you will need two 'purchases' accounts, one called 'Purchases Subject to GST' for inventory items that are subject to the GST and one called 'Purchases GST Free' for GST-free items.

Fortunately, most Australian computerised bookkeeping programs come with a default set of accounts that you simply modify to suit your business's needs. The GST codes used are shown in table 2.12 and the BAS codes in table 2.13.

Table 2.12: GST codes

GST codes	Description	GST codes	Description
GST	GST included in cost	PYE	PAYE deductions
NT	Nonreportable	FBT	Fringe benefits tax
INP	Input taxed amount	WT	Withholding tax
SAL	Salary and wages	PER	Personal use
FRE	GST free		

Table 2.13: BAS codes

BAS codes	Description	BAS codes	Description
G1	Taxable supply	G18	Acquisition adjustment
G2	Export	W1	Wages and salaries

BAS codes	Description	BAS codes	Description
G3	GST free	W2	PAYE
G4	Input taxed supply	W4	Withholding no ABN
G7	Supply adjustment	T1	Income tax
G10	Capital acquisition	F1	Fringe benefits tax
G11	Other acquisition	F2	Fringe benefits tax variation
G13	Input taxed acquisition	NT	Nonreportable
G15	Private use		

Note

Not all business transactions recorded in your ledgers are subject to the GST and often are not required to be included in your BAS. Opening balances, end-of-year adjustments, depreciation and so on are all examples of where the code 'NT (Nonreportable)' would be used or the equivalent in other accounting programs. The code FRE is used for items that do not include the GST, such as basic food stuffs. An example would be milk for the staff coffee. See day 6 for a complete discussion on the BAS and the BAS codes.

Revision exercise for day 2

Analyse the following transactions and create appropriate general journal entries that also take into account any GST implications.

01/02/YY Contributed $10 000 in cash to the business

01/02/YY Took out a business loan of $50 000 repayable in 12 months for working capital

02/02/YY	Bought a truck for the business for $16 500 cash
02/02/YY	Made a cash sale of $345.98
03/02/YY	Paid telephone account of $267.89
04/02/YY	Made a credit sale to Mrs Jones of $325.98
15/02/YY	Purchased inventory for cash $234.12
16/02/YY	Purchased inventory from Mr Smith on credit for $424.12
26/02/YY	Paid myself $897.56
29/02/YY	Paid my creditor of the 16th
30/02/YY	Bought an office desk for cash $645

All amounts include the GST component (you have to also account for GST where applicable). Please do not include any folio numbers or a notation.

Please draw up forms with the following headings, using as many rows as you require. They can also be downloaded from my website <www.tpabusiness.com.au>.

Date	Particulars	Folio	Debit ($)	Credit ($)

Account name: Cash at Bank **Folio number:**

Date	Details	Folio	Debit ($)	Credit ($)	Balance ($)

Account name: Debtor (Mrs Jones) **Folio number:**

Date	Details	Folio	Debit ($)	Credit ($)	Balance ($)

Account name: Motor Vehicle **Folio number:**

Date	Details	Folio	Debit ($)	Credit ($)	Balance ($)

Account name: Office Furniture **Folio number:**

Date	Details	Folio	Debit ($)	Credit ($)	Balance ($)

Account name: Creditor (Mr Smith) **Folio number:**

Date	Details	Folio	Debit ($)	Credit ($)	Balance ($)

Account name: Loan **Folio number:**

Date	Details	Folio	Debit ($)	Credit ($)	Balance ($)

Account name: GST **Folio number:**

Date	Details	Folio	Debit ($)	Credit ($)	Balance ($)

Account name: Capital **Folio number:**

Date	Details	Folio	Debit ($)	Credit ($)	Balance ($)

Account name: Drawings **Folio number:**

Date	Details	Folio	Debit ($)	Credit ($)	Balance ($)

Account name: Sales **Folio number:**

Date	Details	Folio	Debit ($)	Credit ($)	Balance ($)

Account name: Purchases **Folio number:**

Date	Details	Folio	Debit ($)	Credit ($)	Balance ($)

Account name: Telephone **Folio number:**

Date	Details	Folio	Debit ($)	Credit ($)	Balance ($)

Now finally we transfer all of the balances to the trial balance.

Trial Balance

Company name ……………………… **as at** …. / …. / ….

Account #	Account name	Debit ($)	Credit ($)
	TOTALS		

Day 3

Cash receipts and cash payments

Key terms and concepts

- *Cash*: besides meaning actual money, in business cash usually means cheques as well as direct debits and credit card transactions.
- All cash receipts are accounted for in the cash receipts journal.
- All cash payments are accounted for in the cash payments journal.
- When combined, the cash receipts and the cash payments journals are often referred to as the 'cash book'.

In days 1 and 2 we categorised our transactions according to a chart of accounts that we created to suit our own business needs and we recorded our business transactions on a 'one by one' basis, which can be very time-consuming. In this lesson we will learn about **special journals** that make the recording of business transactions a little easier.

Source documents

There are many documents produced by a business entity during your normal business activity that provide the source of information you need to enter into your accounting system.

One of the first steps in starting a new business is to open a bank account, usually a cheque account. When you write a cheque to pay an account or make a purchase it is the cheque stub that is the source of information that you need to enter that payment into your accounting records. An example of how this would appear in a cash payments journal is shown in table 3.1.

Table 3.1: recording cheques in cash payments journal

Date	Chq #	Particulars	Amount (Bank; $)
01/01/09	1234	West Electricty	125.77
03/01/09	1235	Shell Garage	3478.99
05/01/09	1236	Dell Computers	1563.93

Other sources of information that emanate from your cheque account include your bank statement, which will indicate any direct debit payments you may have in place, bank charges and so on.

In the normal course of business you will also receive money for which you may issue a receipt, or receive money directly into your cash register or as a direct deposit into your bank account. The copy of the receipt you issued, your daily cash register total and your bank statement are all sources of information that you will use to enter financial information into your cash receipts journal, as shown in table 3.2.

Table 3.2: recording receipts in cash receipts journal

Date	Receipt #	Particulars	Amount (Bank; $)
01/01/09	Till	Cash sales	2678.55
03/01/09	23987	R Jones	3478.99
05/01/09	Bank	Interest	1.93

There are also invoices that you receive and invoices that you create for inventory bought and sold on credit terms. These will be entered into the purchases and sales journals, as shown in table 3.3. Adjustments notes, for when goods are returned (previously called credit notes), will be the source of information for your returns journals.

Table 3.3: recording invoices in purchases journal

Date	Invoice received	Particulars (creditor's account to be credited)	Accounts payable amount ($)
10/01/09	34195	Smiths Widgets Pty Ltd	29 146.99
10/01/09	500045	Braggings Cold Presses	5654.88

Legal obligations

Only transactions that give rise to a legal obligation are to be entered into your accounting records. If you issue a **purchase order** to buy some stock, you do not enter the details of that purchase until you receive the invoice from your supplier; in other words until your offer to purchase has been accepted and there is a contract between you.

Cash receipts and cash payments

Originally only the general journal was used to record transactions. It soon became obvious, however, that many transactions were being duplicated time and time again. How many times do you pay wages in a given month? Therefore some special journals were created to handle cash receipts and payments in a more efficient manner. Later in this section we will also examine some special journals that record our credit purchases and sales.

The first stage of the change was to summarise the cash transactions from multiline journal entries into one line in the cash journals, as example 3.1 shows.

Example 3.1

01/04/YY Paid wages of $450.00.

If we were to use the general journal, the entry would appear as follows:

Date	Particulars	Folio	Debit ($)	Credit ($)
01/04/YY	Wages	6230	13 530.00	
	Cash at Bank	1100		12 300.00
	Being: Wages for week ending 01/04			

However, in a cash payments journal the payment could appear like this:

Cash Payments Journal **CP1**

Date	Chq #	Particulars	Amount (Bank; $)	Wages ($)
01/04/YY	123	Wages for 01/04	450.00	450.00
		TOTALS		
		FOLIO	Cr	Cr

You will notice that we now only need to record the information on one line.

The next innovation was to post the cash journals only once at the end of each month. If we had five wages payments per month, in a general journal we would need 15 lines posted five times to Wages and five times to the Bank account. This would be even more complex if the expense item involved a GST calculation. As table 3.4 shows, in the cash journals we only need the totals of the five lines posted once to Wages and once to the Bank acccount (and if necessary once to the GST).

Table 3.4: entering information into the cash journal

Cash Payments Journal **CP1**

Date	Chq #	Particulars	Amount (Bank; $)	Wages ($)
01/04/YY	123	Wages for 01/04	450.00	450.00
08/04/YY	124	Wages for 08/04	495.00	495.00
15/04/YY	125	Wages for 15/04	385.00	385.00
22/04/YY	126	Wages for 22/04	743.00	743.00
29/04/YY	127	Wages for 29/04	564.00	564.00
		TOTALS	2637.00	2637.00
		FOLIO	Cr 1100	Dr 6230

Account name: Wages **Folio number: 6230**

Date	Details	Folio	Debit ($)	Credit ($)	Balance ($)
31/04/YY	Wages for April	CP1	2637.00		2637.00

Note

The wages amount is posted only once, as highlighted by the circle.

We are now going to expand our cash receipts and cash payments journals, but not fully at this stage. We will only do that once we have discussed returns and allowances. The forms we will use in these exercises are drawn up as shown in example 3.2.

The columns that you decide to use in your cash payments or cash receipts journals are completely up to you, depending upon the business that you are in. There is really no defined structure for the cash journals. For the purposes of this book the number of columns we indicate is limited by its page width. If you use a spreadsheet program to create your cash journals, you can create as many columns as you require. For an example of a spreadsheet cash journal, see my website <www.tpabusiness.com.au>.

Columns in the cash payments and cash receipts journals are meant to hold details of payments that are made regularly during the month, such as wages paid every week. Where a payment is only made occasionally, such as your quarterly electricity bill, then you would use the Other Payments column to record this. This applies equally to both the cash payments and cash receipts journals. In example 3.2 we will examine a cash payment that only occurs occasionally and therefore doesn't require its own column but is subject to GST. For this we will refer to our Electricity account.

Example 3.2

10/05/YY Paid West Electricity $440 for April's electricity usage.

12/05/YY Paid West Gas $330 for April's gas usage.

Date	Chq #	Particulars	Amount (Bank; $)	GST (paid; $)	Other payments		Folio
					Amount ($)	Details	
10/05/YY	123	West Elec.	440.00	40.00	400.00	Electricity	Dr 6200
12/05/YY	124	West Gas	330.00	30.00	300.00	Gas	Dr 6210
		TOTALS	770.00	70.00	700.00		
		FOLIO	Cr 1100	Dr 2100			

You will notice that the total credit of $770 to the Bank account equals the total debit of the GST and Other Payments accounts, but the Other Payments amounts are all posted separately.

Account name: Bank **Folio number: 1100**

Date	Details	Folio	Debit ($)	Credit ($)	Balance ($)
30/05/YY	May CP	CP1		770.00	(770.00)

Account name: GST **Folio number: 2100**

Date	Details	Folio	Debit ($)	Credit ($)	Balance ($)
30/05/YY	May GST	CP1	70.00		70.00

Account name: Electricity **Folio number: 6200**

Date	Details	Folio	Debit ($)	Credit ($)	Balance ($)
10/05/YY	West Electricity	CP1	400.00		400.00

Account name: Gas **Folio number: 6210**

Date	Details	Folio	Debit ($)	Credit ($)	Balance ($)
12/05/YY	West Gas	CP1	300.00		300.00

You should also note the dates used. The date of entry into the ledger of the totals is the last day of the month, such as the Bank and GST accounts, whereas the Other Payments, such as the Electricity and Gas accounts used in this example, are posted using the actual date of the payment.

Let's now try an exercise.

Exercise 3.1

Post the following transactions to the cash payments and cash receipts journals using the forms drawn up as shown. They can also be downloaded from my website <www.tpabusiness.com.au>.

Jan 08 Cheque 456 Telstra for telephone expense: $300 + $30 GST = $330

Jan 10 Cheque 457 West Electricity for electricity: $100 + $10 GST = $110

Jan 15 Cheque 458 Stores Pty Ltd for inventory: $1500 + $150 GST = $1650

Jan 28 Cheque 459 MyAds for advertising expense: $600 + $60 GST = $660

Jan 29 Cheque 460 Cash for staff wages: $200

Jan 08 Receipt 230 L Smith cash sales: $800 + $80 GST = $880

Jan 10 Received bank interest from WestBank: $430

Jan 15 Receipt 231 R Rogers paid on account: $1000

Jan 29 Receipt 232 R Brown cash sales: $700 + $70 GST = $770

Cash Payments Journal

CP1

Date	Chq #	Particulars	Amount (Bank; $)	Accounts payable ($)	Cash purchases ($)	GST (paid; $)	Other payments		Folio (creditors)
							Amount ($)	Details	
		TOTALS							
		FOLIO							

Cash Receipts Journal

CR1

Date	Rec #	Particulars	Amount (Bank; $)	Accounts receivable ($)	Fees ($)	GST (collected; $)	Other receipts		Folio (debtors)
							Amount ($)	Details	
		TOTALS							
		FOLIO							

Purchases of assets on deposit using part cash, part credit

All cash payments must be accounted for through the cash payments journal, but how do we record a transaction if we purchase an item partly with cash and partly with credit? In this case we'll use the example of the purchase of a Ford Falcon motor vehicle for $36 000 on 20 per cent deposit and the remainder on credit terms from Little Motors.

Firstly we will account for the motor vehicle and GST in full using the general journal, as is shown in table 3.5. Little Motors will be opened as a liability account in its own right—a sundry creditor. It is not considered under Creditors (Accounts Payable) as the purchase did not relate to the credit purchase of inventory.

Table 3.5: accounting for motor vehicle purchase and GST in general journal

General Journal **CP1**

Date	Particulars	Folio	Debit ($)	Credit ($)
10/06/YY	Motor Vehicles	1500	32 400.00	
	GST	2100	3600.00	
	Little Motors	2900		36 000.00
	Being: Ford Falcon bought from Little Motors on credit			

Next we will draw the cheque on Little Motors and enter the cheque details into the cash payments journal, as shown in table 3.6.

Table 3.6: cheque details shown in cash payments journal

Cash Payments Journal **CP1**

Date	Chq #	Particulars	Amount (Bank; $)	GST (paid; $)	Other payments		Folio
					Amount ($)	Details	
10/06/YY	130	Little Motors	7200.00		7200.00	Deposit on MV	Dr 2900

Note

The cash accounting rules as defined by the Tax Office only apply to inventory purchases and sales. Therefore, even though the motor vehicle you purchased is considered a business asset on credit terms, the GST is still available as a tax credit in the period in which you made the purchase. Please refer to day 6 for full details on cash accounting.

Accounts payable and accounts receivable

When you make credit purchases or **credit sales** of inventory, in other words goods for resale, you will make your final settlement payment through the cash payments journal and receive payment for goods sold through the cash receipts journal. These credit purchases and sales are made via the purchases and sales journals where the actual purchase or sale and GST have been accounted for. Therefore, as shown in example 3.3 (overleaf), when you settle your accounts, or receive payment, the amount will go into the Bank and the Accounts Payable or Receivable accounts only—there is no additional GST required.

Example 3.3

06/06/YY Received $330 from J Smith in settlement of his account.

Cash Receipts Journal **CR1**

Date	Rec #	Particulars	Amount (Bank; $)	Accounts receivable ($)	Cash sales ($)	GST (collected; $)
06/06/YY	123	J Smith	330.00	330.00		

Cash sales and cash purchases

Only credit sales and purchases of inventory are accounted for through the sales and purchases journals. All cash sales and purchase of inventory are accounted for through the sash receipts and cash payments journals. In the case of cash sales and cash purchases, you account for both the sale and the GST through the cash receipts and cash payments journals, as shown in example 3.4.

Example 3.4

08/06/YY Bill Jones purchased 100 widgets @ $25 each for cash.

Cash Receipts Journal **CR1**

Date	Rec #	Particulars	Amount (Bank; $)	Accounts receivable ($)	Cash sales ($)	GST (collected; $)
08/06/YY	125	B Jones	2500.00		2250.00	250.00

Business rules regarding the cash book

All cash payments and all cash receipts will be accounted for through the cash books. There are no exceptions. Any amount that is debited or credited to the Bank account will come via the cash book.

It should also be noted that all payments should be via cheque (or EFTPOS or direct debit) and that the use of hard currency should be discouraged. For minor purchases, such as staffroom tea and coffee, a petty cash book should be used.

All receipts should be deposited in full. There should be no deductions or amounts taken from the cash received, irrespective of the reason.

Computerised accounting: spend money/receive money

In a computerised accounting program, the cash amounts are entered through Cash Payments (Spend Money in MYOB) or Cash Receipts (Receive Money in MYOB) modules that, in practice, are very similar to the cash payments and cash receipts journals. However, there are two types of computerised accounting packages. Those named a 'cash book' generally have a data entry screen that mimics the manual cash book, while 'accounting' programs such as MYOB have a 'header' that often looks like a cheque or receipt and has a grid similar to a spreadsheet where you enter in the details, as indicated by the screenshot in figure 3.1 (overleaf).

Figure 3.1: MYOB 'spend money' page

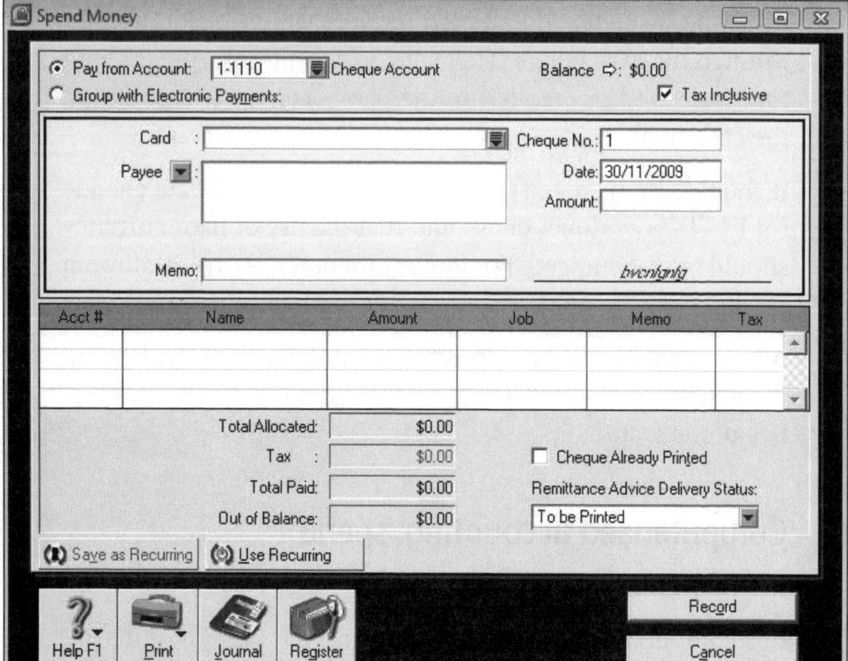

The amounts and details are entered to the correct classifications, a screen of data at a time, similar to a row of data at a time in a manual system, but then like the journal, the posting to the general ledger and the trial balance are automated processes, with the GST calculation also automated. There is no need to post the totals at the end of the month; however, computerised systems still retain the monthly rollover concept as a method of internal control.

The dual use of the cash payments and cash receipts journals and the general journal for some transactions, such as the purchase of a motor vehicle on credit terms with a deposit, is handled the same whether you are using a manual or computerised system.

Revision exercise for day 3

Post the following entries to the appropriate cash payments or cash receipts journals using the same headings as the forms shown overleaf, using as many lines as you require. They can also be downloaded from my website <www.tpabusiness.com.au>.

01/05/YY	Mr Jones started a business by depositing $30 000 into a business cheque account.
02/05/YY	Purchased inventory for $10 000 cash.
03/05/YY	Paid electricity account of $440.
04/05/YY	Paid rent of $1100 (commercial rent includes GST).
05/05/YY	Received ATO refund cheque of $500.
06/05/YY	Bank fees charged of $150.
07/05/YY	Drew $1500 from the business bank account.
08/05/YY	Daily cash sale of $550.
09/05/YY	Paid Widgets & Co $1500 to settle outstanding account.
20/05/YY	Received $1600 from Mr Smith on account.
21/05/YY	Bought computer from My Office for $3300 on 15 per cent deposit.
22/05/YY	Paid rent of $275.
23/05/YY	Cash sales of $990.
24/05/YY	Borrowed $10 000 from WestBank as 'personal' loan. Deposited into cheque account.

Cash Payments Journal

CP1

Date	Chq #	Particulars	Amount (Bank; $)	Accounts payable ($)	Cash purchases ($)	GST (paid; $)	Other payments		Folio (creditors)
							Amount ($)	Details	
		TOTALS							
		FOLIO							

Cash Receipts Journal

CR1

Date	Rec #	Particulars	Amount (Bank; $)	Accounts receivable ($)	Fees ($)	GST (collected; $)	Other receipts		Folio (debtors)
							Amount ($)	Details	
		TOTALS							
		FOLIO							

Now post the amounts that you have entered into your cash book into the appropriate general ledger accounts (using as many as you require) and then prove the posting through a trial balance. You are to allocate names and numbers to the accounts as you deem appropriate.

General Journal **CP1**

Date	Particulars	Folio	Debit ($)	Credit ($)

Account name: **Folio number:**

Date	Details	Folio	Debit ($)	Credit ($)	Balance ($)

Trial Balance
Company Name .... **as at** .... / .... / ....

Account #	Account name	Debit ($)	Credit ($)
	TOTALS		

(Debits must equal the credits)

Day 4

End-of-month reconciliations—proving our transactions

Key terms and concepts

- *Bank reconciliation statement:* the form we use in the process of reconciling your bank statement to your Cash at Bank account.
- You must reconcile your bank statement to your Cash at Bank account on a monthly basis. Before you complete your quarterly BAS, you must ensure that all three months of that quarter have been reconciled. This is a crucial aspect of your bookkeeping process.

So far we have learned how to classify using our chart of accounts, record our transactions into journals and post them to the general ledger accounts, and shortcut that process by using special journals to summarise that data before it is posted to the ledger.

Now we must prove our work. This is done in two ways. Firstly our trial balance will prove that all of our debits equal all of our credits, but, as discussed in this chapter, these amounts will not necessarily all be correct. Secondly, we will prove the bank account data through a process known as the bank reconciliation.

Bank reconciliations

Accounting involves continual cross-checking. When you posted the cash book to the general ledger accounts in the revision exercise in day 3, you double-checked your posting through a trial balance. In the case of a bank reconciliation, we cross-check the details in our ledger's Cash at Bank account to ensure they are correct by comparing them with our bank statement and explaining (reconciling) any differences. We do this *before* we total off and post to the cash book. The 'cash book' is the term we use when referring to the cash payments and cash receipts journals when viewed together.

When you first set up your business cheque account, arrange to receive a bank statement on a regular monthly basis, either electronically or by mail. Your monthly accounts cycle should consist of the following tasks:

- entering cash amounts received or disbursed into your cash book
- checking your bank statement for any amounts not already included in your cash book, such as bank fees and direct debit amounts, and entering them into your cash book
- reconciling your bank account to 'prove' your figures
- totalling your cash book
- posting the totals to your ledger
- double-checking your ledger postings with a trial balance.

You may question why we are attempting to 'reconcile' and not 'equal' our bank account figures. The reason is that it's unlikely your ledger's Cash at Bank account will equal your bank statement balance, even after you have taken into account all of the amounts that were added to your bank statement without your knowledge, such as bank fees and direct debits. The main reasons for this are:

- *unpresented cheques*. When you write a cheque you often use the post to deliver it. The recipient of your cheque then has to deposit it in their bank account. It can then take 15 or more days before the cheque is presented on your bank statement, even though you recorded the cheque in your ledger on the day it was written.
- *outstanding deposits*. The golden rule is that you must deposit all monies received on the day you actually receive them. However, if you use your bank's night safe facility, it is possible that your funds won't be processed until the next working day, which could be the first working day of the following month and hence the possibility of an outstanding deposit appearing on your bank statement.

Note

'Your' bank statement is in fact a copy of the bank's creditors ledger account held in your name. It is the amount of money that it owes you. Therefore, a bank account 'in funds' will show a credit balance (a potential outflow from the bank's viewpoint), whereas a Cash at Bank account in your ledger that is 'in funds' will show a debit balance. In effect you are reconciling your bank statement's credit balance to your accounting record's debit balance, or vice versa.

Reconciling your bank account

After you have recorded all of your receipts and payments for the month in your cash book, ensure you have completed the following steps before you total off.

Step 1: compare your most recent bank reconciliation statement with your bank statement

This **bank reconciliation statement** will undoubtedly contain **unrecorded deposits** and **unpresented cheques**. It is hoped that over the course of the months those amounts will have found their way onto your latest bank statement. Tick off last month's outstanding amounts against this month's bank statement and note any amounts that remain outstanding.

Step 2: cross-check your cash book amounts against your bank statement

Tick off each amount listed in your cash book against the relevant amount on your bank statement. If your cash receipts book doesn't contain a 'Deposited' column, you may have to do some calculations to come up with the bank statement deposits.

Note

It is possible during this process that an error may be detected. For example, a cheque for $140.61 may have been mistakenly entered into your accounts as $160.61. All errors present should be noted and corrected.

Step 3: cross-check your bank statement against your cash book

Examine your bank statement for any amounts that have not been included in your cash book to date, such as bank fees, interest earned or paid, direct debit payments and receipts. Write these amounts into your cash book with the date of entry into the bank statement and the word BANK as the receipt or cheque number. All amounts in your bank statement should now be accounted for in your cash book.

> **Note**
>
> In computerised accounting systems everything that is done in a manual system as described in steps 1 to 3 must be completed electronically. Some systems try to automate the process, such as downloading bank statements in electronic form, but it still remains essentially a 'tick and flick' exercise.

Step 4: complete your bank reconciliation statement

Firstly, take note of any amounts in your cash book that have not been ticked off. These are the outstanding deposits and unpresented cheques that will appear on your bank reconciliation statement. You are now in a position to write up your bank reconciliation statement in the format as shown in figure 4.1 (overleaf).

Figure 4.1: bank reconciliation statement

Bank reconciliation as at … / … / ……			
Closing balance of the bank statement		$	________
Plus outstanding deposit of … / … / ……			
Less unpresented cheques:			
Cheque number	**Amount**		
			________
Closing balance of general ledger Cash at Bank account		$	________

If the closing balance of your bank statement equals your 'calculated' Cash at Bank account balance, you can go ahead and total off and post your cash book. If not, you start again.

The step-by-step process described in this section to reconcile your bank account is shown in example 4.1.

Example 4.1

Our bank reconciliation statement for April is as follows:

Bank reconciliation as at 30/04/20YY				
Closing balance of the bank statement			$	65 864.78
Plus outstanding deposit of 29/04/20YY			$	5 016.01 ✓
Less unpresented cheques:				
Cheque number	**Amount**			
199	2045.78	✓		
122	945.23	✓	$	2 991.01
Closing balance of general ledger Cash at Bank account			$	67 889.78

Our bank statement for May is as follows:

WestBank Ltd

14 Anywhere Street, LinconVille WA 6999

MyBusiness Pty Ltd
PO Box 123
LinconVille WA 6999

May YY
No 56

Date	Particulars	Debit ($)	Credit ($)	Balance ($)		
01/05/YY	Opening balance			65 864.78	Cr	✓
01/05/YY	Deposit		5016.01	70 880.79	Cr	✓
01/05/YY	Transfer		30 000.00	100 880.79	Cr	✓
02/05/YY	Cheque 119	2045.78		98 835.01	Cr	✓
03/05/YY	Cheque 124	440.00		98 395.01	Cr	✓
04/05/YY	Cheque 123	10 000.00		88 395.01	Cr	✓
04/05/YY	Cheque 122	945.23		87 449.78	Cr	✓
05/05/YY	ATO		500.00	87 949.78	Cr	
06/05/YY	Bank fees	150.00		87 799.78	Cr	
08/05/YY	Deposit		550.00	88 349.78	Cr	✓
08/05/YY	Cheque 125	1100.00		87 249.78	Cr	✓
10/05/YY	Cheque 127	1500.00		85 749.78	Cr	✓
21/05/YY	Cheque 126	1500.00		84 249.78	Cr	✓
21/05/YY	Deposit		1600.00	85 849.78	Cr	✓
24/05/YY	Transfer		10 000.00	95 849.78	Cr	✓
24/05/YY	Cheque 129	250.00		95 599.78	Cr	✓

Step 1 is to check that the outstanding amounts from last month's bank reconciliation statement are shown on this month's bank statement.

Step 2 is to tick off our cash book amounts against our bank statement, noting any amounts included in our cash book that are not indicated on the bank statement.

Our cash book written up with known amounts for May appears as follows:

Cash Payments Journal **CP1**

Date	Chq #	Particulars	Amount (Bank; $)	
02/05/YY	123	Cash purchase	10 000.00	✓
03/05/YY	124	West Electricity	440.00	✓
04/05/YY	125	My Landlord	1100.00	✓
07/05/YY	126	J Bloggs	1500.00	✓
09/05/YY	127	Widgets & Co	1500.00	✓
21/05/YY	128	MyOffice Pty Ltd	495.00	
22/05/YY	129	My Landlord	250.00	✓

Cash Receipts Journal **CR1**

Date	Rec #	Particulars	Amount (Bank; $)	
01/05/YY	Bank	Owners	30 000.00	✓
08/05/YY	Till	Cash sales	550.00	✓
20/05/YY	567	Mr Smith	1600.00	✓
23/05/YY	Till	Cash sales	990.00	
24/05/YY	Bank	WestBank	10 000.00	✓

Step 3 is to insert any amounts from our bank statement that have not yet been included in our cash book, such as bank interest or charges and direct debits. Next total off the cash book, which will be presented as follows:

Cash Payments Journal **CP1**

Date	Chq #	Particulars	Amount (Bank; $)	
02/05/YY	123	Cash Purchase	10 000.00	✓
03/05/YY	124	West Electricity	440.00	✓
04/05/YY	125	My Landlord	1 100.00	✓
07/05/YY	126	J Bloggs	1 500.00	✓
09/05/YY	127	Widgets & Co	1 500.00	✓
21/05/YY	128	My Office Pty Ltd	495.00	
22/05/YY	129	My Landlord	250.00	✓
06/05/YY	Bank	Bank Fees	150.00	✓
		TOTALS	15 435.00	
		FOLIO	Cr	

Cash Receipts Journal **CR1**

Date	Rec #	Particulars	Amount (Bank; $)	
01/05/YY	Bank	Owners	30 000.00	✓
08/05/YY	Till	Cash Sales	550.00	✓
20/05/YY	567	Mr Smith	1 600.00	✓
23/05/YY	Till	Cash Sales	990.00	
24/05/YY	Bank	WestBank	10 000.00	✓
05/05/YY	Bank	ATO	500.00	✓
		TOTALS	43 640.00	
		FOLIO	Dr	

Step 4 is to write up our bank reconciliation statement, which will look like the figure overleaf:

Bank reconciliation as at 31/05/20YY

Closing balance of the bank statement		**$**	**95 599.78 cr**
***Plus* outstanding deposit of 23/05/20YY**		**$**	**990.00**
***Less* unpresented cheques:**			
Cheque number	**Amount**		
128	495.00	**$**	**495.00**
Closing balance of general ledger Cash at Bank account		**$**	**96 094.78 dr**

Opening Balance as per last Bank Rec	$67 889.78
Plus Deposits	$43 640.00
Less Payments	$15 435.00
	$96 094.78

As the bank reconciliation now balances, we can total off our cash book and post the totals to our general ledger accounts and verify our posting through a trial balance. At the end of this process our Cash at Bank account will look like the following:

Account name: Cash at Bank **Folio number: 1100**

Date	Details	Folio	Debit ($)	Credit ($)	Balance ($)
01/05/YY	Opening Balance		67 889.78		67 889.78
31/05/YY	Cash Deposits	CR1	43 640.00		111 529.78
31/05/YY	Cash Receipts	CP1		15 435.00	96 094.78

For an opportunity to complete a bank reconciliation yourself, try exercise 4.1.

Exercise 4.1

Enter the following transactions into the appropriate *abbreviated* cash payments or cash receipts journals for June using the same headings as in the forms shown, using as many lines as you require. Next post the bank totals to the Cash at Bank account and finally write up a bank reconciliation statement.

02/02/YY	Made a cash sale of $345.98.
02/06/YY	Cheque 130 Purchased inventory for $11 000 cash.
03/06/YY	Cheque 131 Paid electricity account of $440.
04/06/YY	Cheque 132 Paid rent of $990.
07/06/YY	Cheque 133 Drew $1500 from the business bank account.
08/06/YY	Daily cash sale of $550.
09/06/YY	Cheque 134 Paid Widgets & Co $2200 to settle outstanding account.
22/06/YY	Cheque 135 Paid rent of $990.
23/06/YY	Cash sales of $1980.
24/06/YY	Cheque 136 Paid wages costing $3300.
28/06/YY	Cash sales of $880.

Our bank statement for June appears as follows:

WestBank Ltd

14 Anywhere Street, LinconVille WA 6999

MyBusiness Pty Ltd
PO Box 123
LinconVille WA 6999

June YY
No 57

Date	Particulars	Debit ($)	Credit ($)	Balance ($)	
01/06/YY	Opening Balance			95 599.78	Cr
01/06/YY	Deposit		990.00	96 589.78	Cr
04/06/YY	Cheque 130	11 000.00		85 589.78	Cr
06/06/YY	Cheque 132	990.00		84 599.78	Cr
07/06/YY	Cheque 133	1 500.00		83 099.78	Cr
09/06/YY	Deposit		550.00	83 649.78	Cr
13/06/YY	Interest on Deposit		1 200.00	84 849.78	Cr
15/06/YY	Cheque 131	440.00		84 409.78	Cr
15/06/YY	BHP Dividend		1 256.00	85 665.78	Cr
24/06/YY	Deposit		1 980.00	87 645.78	Cr
24/06/YY	Cheque 136	3 300.00		84 345.78	Cr
27/06/YY	Cheque 135	990.00		83 355.78	Cr
29/06/YY	Bank Fee	66.00		83 289.78	Cr

Cash Payments Journal **CP1**

Date	Chq #	Particulars	Amount (Bank; $)
		TOTALS	
		FOLIO	Cr

Cash Receipts Journal **CR1**

Date	Rec #	Particulars	Amount (Bank; $)
		TOTALS	
		FOLIO	Dr

Account name: Cash at Bank **Folio number: 1100**

Date	Details	Folio	Debit ($)	Credit ($)	Balance ($)
01/06/YY	Opening balance		96 094.78		96 094.78

Bank Reconciliation as at … / … / ……

Closing balance of the bank statement $ ________

Plus **outstanding deposit of … / … / ……**

Less **unpresented cheques:**

Cheque number **Amount**

____

Closing balance of general ledger Cash at Bank account $ ________

Note

Dividends are usually 'franked'; that is, they carry with them a tax credit. You'll need to inform your accountant of this, but from a bookkeeping viewpoint the franking credit is ignored.

Computerised accounting

Performing a bank reconciliation in a computerised accounting program is very similar to the manual process. It still requires you to 'tick off' the cash entries against your bank statement and to input any information contained in your bank statement that is not included in your records. The actual process to complete the bank reconciliation is a little easier, but on the whole it's still a fairly labour-intensive manual process. The screenshot in figure 4.2 shows a default bank reconciliation form.

Figure 4.2: computerised accounting program bank reconciliation form

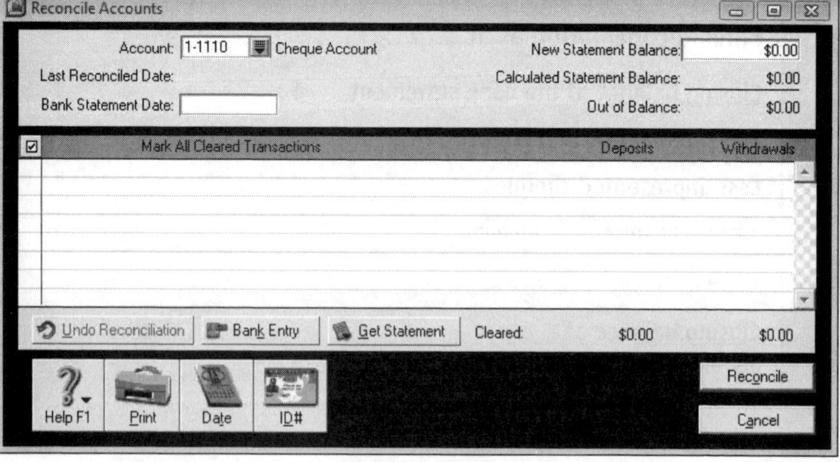

Some accounting packages allow you to download your bank statement into your accounting system to make the process a little easier. This can be useful, but it's still important that you familiarise yourself with the manual process first so that you fully understand what your computerised accounting program is trying to do.

Revision exercise for day 4

Using the forms as shown, post the following transactions to the appropriate *abbreviated* cash payments or cash receipts journals for July. Next post the bank totals to the Cash at Bank account and then finally write up a bank reconciliation statement.

02/07/YY	Cheque 137 Purchased inventory for $9000 cash.
03/07/YY	Cheque 138 Paid electricity account of $330.
04/07/YY	Cheque 139 Drew $1500 from the business bank account.
05/07/YY	Cheque 140 Paid rent of $990.
08/07/YY	Daily cash sale of $660.
22/07/YY	Cheque 141 Paid rent of $990.
23/07/YY	Cash sales of $330.
24/07/YY	Cheque 142 Paid wages costing $3300.
28/07/YY	Cash sales of $1650.

Note

This revision exercise carries on from the data recorded in exercise 4.1 but it also crosses the financial year's end. This is to emphasise that there is no 'year's end' for bank reconciliations. They just flow from one month to the other.

Our bank statement for July appears as follows:

WestBank Ltd

14 Anywhere Street, LinconVille WA 6999

MyBusiness Pty Ltd **July YY**
PO Box 123 **No 58**
LinconVille WA 6999

Date	Particulars	Debit ($)	Credit ($)	Balance ($)	
01/07/YY	Opening Balance			83 289.78	Cr
01/07/YY	Deposit		880.00	84 169.78	Cr
04/07/YY	Cheque 137	9 000.00		75 169.78	Cr
06/07/YY	Cheque 138	330.00		74 839.78	Cr
06/07/YY	Cheque 128	495.00		74 344.78	Cr
07/07/YY	Cheque 134	2 200.00		72 144.78	Cr
07/7/YY	Cheque 139	1 500.00		70 644.78	Cr
09/07/YY	Deposit		660.00	71 304.78	Cr
09/07/YY	Cheque 140	990.00		70 314.78	Cr
24/07/YY	Deposit		330.00	70 644.78	Cr
27/07/YY	Cheque 142	3 300.00		67 344.78	Cr
29/07/YY	Bank Fee	66.00		67 278.78	Cr

Cash Payments Journal **CP1**

Date	Chq #	Particulars	Amount (Bank; $)
		TOTALS	
		FOLIO	Cr

Cash Receipts Journal **CR1**

Date	Rec #	Particulars	Amount (Bank; $)
		TOTALS	
		FOLIO	Dr

Account name: Cash at Bank **Folio number: 1100**

Date	Details	Folio	Debit ($)	Credit ($)	Balance ($)
01/05/YY	Opening Balance		81 474.78		81 474.78

Bank reconciliation as at … / … / ……

Closing balance of the bank statement $________

***Plus* outstanding deposit of … / … / ……**

***Less* unpresented cheques:**

Cheque number **Amount**

____

Closing balance of general ledger Cash at Bank account $________

Day 5

The purchase and sale of inventory on credit terms

Key terms and concepts

- *Inventory:* goods that we purchase for resale. It is the basis of our business and is not something used or consumed within our business itself.
- *Credit purchase and credit sale:* a purchase or sale of inventory where settlement of the account occurs at a later time. The credit terms are usually stated on the invoice, for example, 'Net 30 days'.
- *Accrual accounting: r*ecording of all business transactions at the time that a legal obligation exists for you to pay or receive money, albeit sometime in the future. You 'accrue' or record the right within your accounting system.
- *'Cash accounting' principles:* under cash accounting rules, credit purchases and credit sales are only recorded in the accounting system on settlement (or part settlement) of the account.
- The Purchase and Sales journals are only for use for the credit purchase or credit sale of inventory.

- The Purchases and Sales entries within the cash book are for cash purchases and cash sales only, but we may have to modify this rule for credit purchases and credit sales that are to be accounted for on a cash basis.

Today we are going to learn how to account for credit sales and credit purchases. We are also going to examine how to account for the return of goods to our supplier or when our customers return goods to us in both cash and credit situations. We will discuss discounts, both at the time of sale or purchase, or at a later date. We will then re-examine all of this from a cash accounting perspective.

Not all accounting procedures apply universally to all businesses. If your business doesn't involve buying or selling goods or services on credit terms, you can skip this chapter and move on to day 6.

So far, we have looked at the general journal and the cash payments and cash receipts journals. We found that entering transactions through the general journal was a cumbersome process, as was the posting of every transaction to the general ledger.

The cash payments and cash receipts journals made this process easier when the transaction involved cash. By using these journals we could streamline the data entry into one record rather than using multiple lines in the general journal, and we were only required to post the total once per month.

In this chapter we will look at another set of special journals the purchases and sales journals. These journals are used to record the purchase and sale (and returns) of goods purchased on credit for resale at a profit. Goods purchased for resale are called inventory items.

However, you only record in the purchases and sales journals goods purchased on credit for resale—inventory items. Please note the two conditions—inventory and credit terms. Your purchase must relate to inventory and not to other credit purchases, such as a motor vehicle, and the purchase must be on credit terms. Inventory purchased or sold for cash is instead recorded through the cash payments and cash receipts journals respectfully. See example 5.1, which describes purchases and sales for cash.

Example 5.1

On 10 June I make a cash purchase of 10 widgets at $55.00 each from Widgets & Co using cheque number 789.

Cash Payments Journal **CP1**

Date	Chq #	Particulars	Amount (Bank; $)	Cash purchases ($)	GST (paid; $)
10/06/YY	789	Widgets & Co	550.00	500.00	50.00

On 15 June I on sell the widgets to B Smith at a 50 per cent mark-up using receipt number 234.

Cash Receipts Journal **CR1**

Date	Rec #	Particulars	Amount (Bank; $)	Cash sales ($)	GST (collected; $)
15/06/YY	234	B Smith	825.00	750.00	75.00

The purchase and sale has been handled completely within the cash payments and cash receipts journals. For a cash purchase, you credit the Cash at Bank account and debit the Purchases and GST accounts; for a cash sale, you debit the Cash at Bank account and credit the Sales and GST accounts.

Credit purchases and credit sales under accrual accounting

The basic condition for recording any transaction under International Accounting Standards is that all transactions are recorded at the time that the obligation is cast, that is, at the time that the contract is made, when you have a legal obligation to pay or receive monetary value, albeit some time in the future. If you make a purchase or sale on credit terms, you create mutual obligations at the time the contract for the purchase or sale was entered into, but the payment for that inventory item is delayed under the contract. For example, if your invoice reads 'Net 30 days', it means that you have 30 days to settle the account in full.

You use the purchases or sales journals to record a purchase or sale transaction entered into on a credit basis.

The purchases journal

The purchases journal is used to record credit purchases under the **accrual accounting** system. The format of a purchases journal is shown in table 5.1.

Table 5.1: purchases journal form

Purchases Journal **PJ1**

Date	Invoice	Particulars (creditor's acct to be debited)	Creditors ledger folio	Accounts payable ($)	Credit purchases ($)	GST (paid; $)
			TOTALS			
			FOLIO	Cr	Dr	Dr

When you make a credit purchase there is no cash transaction, instead you make a promise to pay for these goods at a later date. Therefore you must create a liability account called an Accounts Payable account (**Creditors Control** or **Trade Creditors** account to use alternative names) to which you credit the amount you will pay in the future rather than crediting the Cash at Bank account direct. Note that the inventory purchased is debited to a Purchases account in the cost of goods sold category and not directly to an inventory account.

However, the Accounts Payable (Creditors Control) account is only a **control account**, that is, it only contains total amounts. If our supplier was to query our payment, how could we prove what we owe? The answer is that we also have to keep separate records of our individual supplier's transactions. These separate records are collectively called the creditors ledger, which is a collection of all of the individual creditors accounts. The total of all of the creditors accounts, the creditors ledger summary, is 'reconciled'. An example of an individual creditor's account is shown in table 5.2.

Table 5.2: creditors ledger form

Creditors Ledger (details of our suppliers of inventory on credit)

Creditor's name **CL1**

Date	Details	Folio	Debit ($)	Credit ($)	Balance ($)

When you finally pay the account, you will debit the Accounts Payable account and credit the Cash at Bank account. This is done through your cash payments journal. You will also debit the individual creditor's account.

As shown in table 5.3, when you pay the account through your cash payments journal there is no further GST involved. That was already debited along with the Purchases account in the purchases journal at the time that you recorded the original transaction.

Table 5.3: cash payments journal indicating no GST category

Cash Payments Journal **CP1**

Date	Chq #	Particulars	Amount (Bank; $)	Accounts payable ($)	Folio

See example 5.2, which describes both a purchase and a settlement on credit terms as well as a purchase on credit terms with a deposit paid.

Example 5.2

In the first part of this example we will examine a purchase and settlement on credit terms.

On 10 June I purchase 10 widgets at $55.00 each from Widgets & Co on credit terms to be paid with 14 days. Widget's invoice number 888 confirms this as follows:

Purchases Journal **PJ1**

Date	Invoice	Particulars (creditor's acct to be debited)	Creditors ledger folio	Accounts payable ($)	Credit purchases ($)	GST (paid; $)
10/06/YY	888	Widgets & Co	CL1	550.00	500.00	50.00

The Accounts Payable account was credited with the amount payable in the future and the Purchases and GST accounts were debited. However, the individual creditor's account, as shown following, also has to be credited with the amount:

Creditors Ledger

Creditor's name Widgets & Co **CL1**

Date	Details	Folio	Debit ($)	Credit ($)	Balance ($)
10/06/YY	Invoice 888	PJ1		550.00	(550.00)

On 14 June we settled the account with cheque number 789. We did this through the cash payments journal, as the following example shows:

Cash Payments Journal **CP1**

Date	Chq #	Particulars	Amount (Bank; $)	Accounts payable ($)	Folio
14/06/YY	789	Widgets & Co	550.00	550.00	CL1

This action will credit the Cash at Bank account with the $550.00 (as part of the total posted at the end of the month) and debit the Accounts Payable account with the $550.00 (again in bulk at the end of the month). However, we will also have to credit the individual creditor's account so that the individual's amount outstanding is correct and the total of all creditors ledger accounts equals the Accounts Payable account, as indicated following:

Creditors Ledger

Creditor's name Widgets & Co **CL1**

Date	Details	Folio	Debit ($)	Credit ($)	Balance ($)
10/06/YY	Invoice 888	PJ1		550.00	(550.00)
14/06/YY	Remittance 789	CP1	550.00		0.00

Now we will examine a purchase on credit terms with a deposit paid.

If we were to purchase 100 widgets at $50 each with a 20 per cent deposit, we would first enter the credit purchase in full through the purchases journal and then enter the cheque made out for the deposit in the cash payments journal. In this way the purchases journal records the full details of the purchase and the cash payments journal simply writes off the debt outstanding, as shown following:

Purchases Journal **PJ1**

Date	Invoice	Particulars (creditor's acct to be debited)	Creditors ledger folio	Accounts payable ($)	Credit purchases ($)	GST (paid; $)
10/06/YY	888	Widgets & Co	CL1	550.00	500.00	50.00

Cash Payments Journal **CP1**

Date	Chq #	Particulars	Amount (Bank; $)	Accounts payable ($)	Folio
10/06/YY	789	Widgets & Co	110.00	110.00	CL1

Creditors Ledger

Creditor's name Widgets & Co **CL1**

Date	Details	Folio	Debit ($)	Credit ($)	Balance ($)
10/06/YY	Invoice 888	PJ1		550.00	(550.00)
10/06/YY	Deposit 20% 789	CP1	110.00		(440.00)

The sales journal

The sales journal is used to record credit sales under the accrual accounting system. The format of a sales journal is shown in table 5.4.

Table 5.4: sales journal form

Sales Journal **SJ1**

Date	Invoice	Particulars (debitor's acct to be debited)	Debtors ledger folio	Accounts receivable ($)	Credit sales ($)	GST (collected; $)
			TOTALS			
			FOLIO	Dr	Cr	Cr

When you make a credit sale there is no cash transaction, instead your customer promises to pay for these goods at a later date. Therefore you must create an asset account called an Accounts Receivable account (or **Debtors Control** or Trade Debtors account to use alternative names) to which you debit the amount you hope to receive in the future rather than debiting the Cash at Bank account direct. Note that the inventory sold is credited to the Sales account in the revenue category and is not credited directly to an inventory account. Inventory accounting is something that happens after the trial balance stage and is part of the accounting function rather than the transactional recording bookkeeping function.

However, as with credit purchases, the Accounts Receivable account is only a 'control' account, that is, it only contains total amounts. If our customer was to query our request for payment, how could we prove the debt? The answer is that we also have to keep separate records of our individual customer's transactions. These separate records are collectively called the debtors ledger, that is, a collection of all of the individual debtor's accounts. The total of all of the debtors accounts, the debtors ledger summary, is 'reconciled' back to the Accounts Receivable (Debtors Control) account at regular intervals.

An example of an individual debtor's account is shown in table 5.5.

Table 5.5: debtors ledger form

Debtors Ledger (details of our 'credit' customers)

Debtor's name **DL1**

Date	Details	Folio	Debit ($)	Credit ($)	Balance ($)

When you are finally paid, you will debit the Cash at Bank account and credit the Accounts Receivable account. This is done through your cash receipts journal. You will also be required to credit the individual debtor's account.

As shown in table 5.6. you will notice once again that when you receive the payment, there is no further GST involved. That was already credited along with the Sales account in the sales journal at the time that you recorded the original credit sale.

Table 5.6: cash receipts journal indicating no GST category

Cash Receipts Journal **CR1**

Date	Rec #	Particulars	Amount (Bank; $)	Accounts receivable ($)	Folio

See example 5.3, which describes both a sale and a settlement on credit terms as well as a sale on credit terms with a deposit paid.

Example 5.3

In the first part of this example we will examine a sale and settlement on credit terms.

The first rule of selling on credit terms is to vet your customers and make sure that they a good credit risk.

On 15 June I on-sell the widgets to B Smith at a 50 per cent markup using invoice number 987, stipulating that the account is to be settled within 14 days:

Sales Journal **SJ1**

Date	Invoice	Particulars (debitor's acct to be debited)	Debtors ledger folio	Accounts receivable ($)	Credit sales ($)	GST (collected; $)
15/06/YY	987	B Smith	D1	825.00	750.00	75.00

The Accounts Receivable account was debited with the amount owed and the Sales and GST accounts were credited. However, the individual debtor's account, as shown following, also has to be debited with the amount:

Debtors Ledger

Debtor's name B Smith **DL1**

Date	Details	Folio	Debit ($)	Credit ($)	Balance ($)
15/06/YY	Invoice 987	SJ1	825.00		825.00

On 21 June B Smith sends us a cheque for $825.00.

Cash Receipts Journal **CR1**

Date	Rec #	Particulars	Amount (Bank; $)	Accounts receivable ($)	Folio
21/06/YY		B Smith	825.00	825.00	D1

This action will debit the Cash at Bank account with Mr Smith's $825.00 (as part of the total posted at the end of the month) and credit the Accounts Receivable account with the $825.00 (again in bulk at the end of the month). However, we will also have to debit the individual debtor's account so that the individual's amount outstanding is correct and the total of all the debtors ledgers equals the Accounts Receivable account, as indicated following:

Debtors Ledger

Debtor's name B Smith **DL1**

Date	Details	Folio	Debit ($)	Credit ($)	Balance ($)
15/06/YY	Invoice 987	SJ1	825.00		825.00
21/06/YY	Cash receipt	CR1		825.00	0

Now we will examine a sale on credit terms with a deposit paid.

If we on-sold the 100 widgets at $75 each with a 20 per cent deposit, we would first enter the credit sale in full through the sales journal and then enter the monies received for the deposit in the cash receipts journal. In this way the sales journal records the full details of the credit sale and the cash receipts journal simply writes off the debt outstanding. This is exactly the same procedure as for purchases on credit terms with a deposit paid, as outlined in example 5.2.

In exercise 5.1 Mr Jones is going to book and pay for a cruise on credit terms. This will demonstrate the complexity of using a manual system for these types of transactions.

Exercise 5.1

Our business is a travel agency called MyTravel. A customer, Mr Jones, wishes to purchase a return ticket for a cruise on the *Western Sun* leaving Fremantle on 30 October for Bunbury, Albany and Esperance. The ticket will cost Mr Jones $2640 for which he will make a 50 per cent deposit. We will order the ticket from Western Sun Ticketing on a 25 per cent deposit, with the remainder to be paid two weeks before sailing. We mark up the cost by 33.3 per cent to arrive at the price we have charged Mr Jones.

Mr Jones also wishes to book three tours, one in each city visited, from City Tours. The tours can be requested, but not confirmed until 14 days before sailing when 100 per cent payment is required. The tours cost us $600 each, to which we will add a 33.3 per cent mark-up.

Referring to the situation just described, analyse the following circumstances and answer the questions indicated by calculating the amounts involved and creating the appropriate journal entries in the forms drawn up as shown.

2 Oct YY Mr Jones pays a deposit of $1320 for the ticket on the *Western Sun*. He also requests three tours with City Tours to be included.

Ticket cost: *GST:* *Deposit:*

3 Oct YY Western Sun Ticketing confirms the availability and issues an invoice. We pay a 25 per cent deposit.

Our cost: *GST:* *Deposit:*

4 Oct YY City Tours accepts our booking for Mr Jones subject to sufficient numbers.

What is required of us?

Why?

7 Oct YY City Tours confirms the Albany and Bunbury tours but the Esperance tour is cancelled due to insufficient numbers. We receive its invoice. Mr Jones is informed and asked to make his final payment.

Our cost: *GST:* *Deposit:*

10 Oct YY Final settlement is received from Mr Jones.

Cost of cruise: *Cost of tours:*

14 Oct YY Final payment is made to Western Sun Ticketing and City Tours.

Cost of cruise: *Cost of tours:*

Sales Journal **SJ1**

Date	Invoice	Particulars (debtor's acct to be debited)	Debtors ledger folio	Accounts receivable ($)	Credit sales ($)	GST (collected; $)

Cash Receipts Journal **CR1**

Date	Rec #	Particulars	Amount (Bank; $)	Accounts receivable ($)	Folio

Purchases Journal PJ1

Date	Invoice	Particulars (creditor's acct to be debited)	Creditors ledger folio	Accounts payable ($)	Credit Purchases ($)	GST (paid; $)

Cash Payments Journal CP1

Date	Chq #	Particulars	Amount (Bank; $)	Accounts payable ($)	Folio

Debtors Ledger

Debtor's name Mr Jones DL1

Date	Details	Folio	Debit ($)	Credit ($)	Balance ($)

Creditors Ledger

Creditor's name Western Sun Ticketing CL1

Date	Details	Folio	Debit ($)	Credit ($)	Balance ($)

Creditors Ledger

Creditor's name City Tours **CL1**

Date	Details	Folio	Debit ($)	Credit ($)	Balance ($)

Returns and allowances under accrual accounting

Have you ever bought a pair of shoes and later decided that you didn't like them and then returned them to the store? This is a classic example of a return, but in business such returns are a little more complex. For example, if a stock line is not selling, instead of returning the goods you may seek a discount from the supplier. This is referred to as an allowance.

Returning goods purchased or sold

At some time we have all purchased an item that we have later returned for one reason or another. Returns of goods purchased, or returns to us of goods sold by us, are readily identified by the average consumer.

If you purchased/sold the goods on cash terms, you would simply receive/pay a cash refund processed through the cash receipts and cash payments journal. The document you would receive/issue is called an **adjustment note** (credit note) and is in all ways similar to a tax invoice, but with a negative cost indicated rather than a positive one. Since the introduction of the GST, the term 'adjustment note' is used rather than the older term 'credit note' because the return is handled as an adjustment in your BAS; however, many small companies treat returns as negative purchases/sales and simply show the net amount in the BAS. Either way is acceptable for returns within the BAS period but for out-of-period returns, the adjustment method is preferred.

If you purchased/sold the goods on credit terms, there are two scenarios that we have to cover. If the goods have been paid for and the account settled, the return is usually settled as a cash payment similar to the process just described for goods purchased/sold on cash terms, or alternatively as a credit settlement with the individual creditor's/debtor's account going into negative—to be utilised as a credit on the next purchase/sale. Which one you use will depend on whether or not the return relates to a supplier/customer with whom you have regular dealings, or if the transaction is just a one off. Sometimes the terms of trade will also dictate the type of refund given on returned goods.

Note

With regard to terms of trade, in both situations just described it is possible that the terms of trade will dictate that an adjustment note will be issued and that no cash refund will be given. Such terms are only legal for voluntary returns, that is, when the client changes its mind. In cases of statutory returns, that is, the return of goods under consumer law, a cash refund must be given if the purchase/sale was for cash, or if on credit terms and the account has been settled prior to the return taking place.

If the purchase or sale return is via an adjustment note, which itself is on credit terms, a purchases (or sales) returns and allowances journal is used, as shown by the forms indicated in tables 5.7 and 5.8.

Table 5.7: purchases returns and allowances journal form

Purchases Returns and Allowances Journal **PR1**

Date	Adjustment note	Particulars (creditor's acct to be debited)	Creditors ledger folio	Accounts payable ($)	Credit purchases returns ($)	GST (adjustment; ($)
			TOTALS			
			FOLIO	Dr	Cr	Cr

Table 5.8: sales returns and allowances journal form

Sales Returns and Allowances Journal **SR1**

Date	Adjustment note	Particulars (debtor's acct to be credited)	Debtors ledger folio	Accounts receivable ($)	Credit sales returns ($)	GST (adjustment; ($)
			TOTALS			
			FOLIO	Dr	Cr	Cr

See example 5.4, which outlines a purchase through a purchases journal followed by a purchases return via an adjustment note processed through a purchases returns and allowances journal.

Example 5.4

On 16 June Mr Smith purchased inventory from Widgets & Co for $1760 using invoice number 1234, as indicated following:

Purchases Journal **PJ1**

Date	Invoice	Particulars (creditor's acct to be debited)	Creditors ledger folio	Accounts payable ($)	Credit purchases ($)	GST (paid; $)
16/06/YY	1234	Widgets & Co	CL1	1760.00	1600.00	160.00

On 25 June the goods arrived, but as they were the wrong colour, Mr Smith returned the goods and received an adjustment note numbered 8765:

Purchases Returns and Allowances Journal **PR1**

Date	Adjustment note	Particulars (creditor's acct to be debited)	Creditors ledger folio	Accounts payable ($)	Credit purchases returns ($)	GST (adjustment; $)
25/06/YY	8765	Widgets & Co	CL1	1760.00	1600.00	160.00

Creditors Ledger

Creditor's name Widgets & Co **CL1**

Date	Details	Folio	Debit ($)	Credit ($)	Balance ($)
16/06/YY	Invoice 1234	PJ1		1760.00	(1760.00)
25/06/YY	Adjustment Note 8765		1760.00		0.00

Applying discounts and allowances

Discounts and allowances received and given is a much misunderstood concept. When you negotiate the original purchase or sale, it doesn't matter in the slightest how the sale value is arrived at—the price settled is the amount you record. The fact that the amount arrived at may have included an 'allowance'—for example, trade, volume or mates' rates reductions—does not influence the fact that only the final figure is reflected in your original purchases or sales journals. All negotiated allowances built into that figure are ignored, *except* any allowance that may be triggered after the contract date, such as an early settlement discount.

The only allowance you should record is an allowance that is triggered or negotiated after the contract price has been settled. For example, if we order goods by sample and what is delivered is not of sample quality, we then have the choice of returning the goods and receiving an adjustment note, or renegotiating and paying a lower invoice value.

All allowances are recorded through the cash payments and cash receipts journals at the time of settlement of the account, as shown by the forms indicated in tables 5.9 and 5.10.

Table 5.9: cash payments journal form

Cash Payments Journal **CP1**

Date	Chq #	Particulars	Amount (Bank; $)	Discount received ($)	GST (adjustment; $)	Accounts payable ($)
		TOTALS				
		FOLIO	Cr	Cr	Cr	Dr

Table 5.10: cash receipts journal form

Cash Receipts Journal **CR1**

Date	Rec #	Particulars	Amount (Bank; $)	Discount allowed ($)	GST (adjustment; $)	Accounts receivable ($)
		TOTALS				
		FOLIO	Dr	Dr	Dr	Cr

In example 5.5 a purchase of inventory is followed by a negotiated adjustment to the purchase price.

Example 5.5

On 16 June Mr Smith purchased inventory from Widgets & Co for $1760 using invoice number 1234.

Purchases Journal **PJ1**

Date	Invoice	Particulars (creditor's acct to be debited)	Creditors ledger folio	Accounts payable ($)	Credit purchases ($)	GST (paid; $)
16/06/YY	1234	Widgets & Co	CL1	1760.00	1600.00	160.00

On 25 June the goods arrived but were the wrong colour. Mr Smith negotiated a 25 per cent discount on the original cost and received an adjustment note numbered 8765. He settled the account using cheque number 456.

Original cost	$1600 plus $160 GST
Adjusted cost	$1200 plus $120 GST
Adjustment note	$400 plus $40 GST

Cash Payments Journal **CP1**

Date	Chq #	Particulars	Amount (Bank; $)	Discount received ($)	GST (adjustment; $)	Accounts payable ($)
25/06/YY	456	Widgets & Co	1320.00	400.00	40.00	1760.00

Creditors Ledger

Creditor's name Widgets & Co CL1

Date	Details	Folio	Debit ($)	Credit ($)	Balance ($)
16/06/YY	Invoice 1234	PJ1		1760.00	(1760.00)
25/06/YY	Adjustment Note 8765		440.00		(1320.00)
25/06/YY	Cheque 456		1320.00		0.00

You will notice that an allowance or discount given after the time of purchase or sale is not only an adjustment to the contract price but also requires a GST adjustment, hence the term 'adjustment note' rather than just a 'credit note' indicating an adjustment to the price only.

Computerised accounting under accrual accounting

It's fairly evident that accounting for purchases and sales on credit terms is a very complex process. This is exacerbated even more when we add returns and allowances into the mix and then top it all off with GST considerations.

The complexity of the manual **accounting process** is in stark contrast to the computerised approach. The source documents involved in the process are the purchase order, invoice and payment advice. The *usual* computerised approach is to create a separate module that handles credit purchases and sales that is tied in very closely to the inventory management system and processes and records the transactions, both from an inventory management and general ledger perspective, as part of the purchase order, invoice and payment advice creation process.

For example, when you receive a purchase request from a customer, you enter the details into the system, which in turn generates an invoice and a warehouse packing slip and updates the inventory record as well as the Accounts Receivable Control account in the general ledger and the individual debtor's account. If an item is not in stock, the system generates the purchase order to your supplier and marks the customer's invoice as goods on back order.

When the goods arrive, the system generates a new invoice and warehouse packing slip and again updates the inventory record as well as the Accounts Receivable Control account and the individual debtor's account.

Similarly, if goods are returned or allowances given, the adjustment note creation processes updates all of the relevant inventory management and general ledger accounts.

Any small business that does any of its transactions on credit terms and uses accrual accounting would be well advised to consider computerised accounting. If you deal primarily with cash, the difference between a computerised and manual approach is not that significant.

Credit purchases and credit sales under cash accounting

If we are a small business entity that has elected to account for our GST liability and our income tax on a cash basis but we also have credit transactions, that is, we purchase and sell inventory on a credit basis, how do we account for credit transactions in cash-based accounting records?

This is a dilemma! There are three ways that we can record our credit transactions. We already know that we can record them when they occur, as is required using the accrual accounting method, or when the account is settled using the cash accounting rules permitted by the Tax Office (ATO). But we can also record the transactions as they take place and then adjust our records to reflect the Tax Office's cash accounting rules for BAS and end-of-year income tax requirements; however, this requires a lot of unnecessary duplication and effort.

The answer to our dilemma lies in the International Accounting Standards themselves (actual title being '**International Financial Reporting Standards**'). So who do we report to? In financial accounting terms we report to ourselves, as the owners of the business. So if we are reporting to ourselves and not to an outside independent owner (shareholder), it is my opinion that we can safely ignore the standards and adopt the Tax Office's cash accounting rules.

A word of caution: we can adopt the Tax Office's cash accounting rules if the business concerned is a small business entity with a turnover under $2 million and no overseas (hedging) transactions. If you are involved in overseas transactions, you may be required to follow International Accounting Standards in order to comply with the Tax Office requirements.

Credit purchases accounted for under cash accounting

When we make a credit purchase—that is, we receive goods with an invoice to be paid sometime in the future—we will update the individual creditor's account with the details of the purchase, but we will not include any details of the purchase or GST in our accounting records; in other words, we will not update the Accounts Payable (Creditors Control) account with the total of our creditors ledger. In fact, we do not even have an account called Accounts Payable in our general ledger accounts.

Example 5.6 outlines a purchase on credit terms using cash accounting (example 5.2 revisited).

Example 5.6

On 10 June I purchased 10 widgets at $55.00 each from Widgets & Co on credit terms to be paid with 14 days.

In this case we don't enter the details in the purchases journal but rather we enter the details directly into our individual creditor's account:

Creditors Ledger

Creditor's name Widgets & Co **CL1**

Date	Details	Folio	Debit ($)	Credit ($)	Balance ($)
10/06/YY	10 Widgets @ $550	888		550.00	(550.00)

The summary of all creditors outstanding is normally reconciled to the Accounts Payable account; however, in this case we do not have such an account and therefore the only record of our total outstanding creditor liabilities is the creditors ledger summary.

On 14 June we settled the account with cheque number 789. We did this through the cash payments journal, as the following example shows:

Cash Payments Journal **CP1**

Date	Chq #	Particulars	Amount (Bank; $)	Cash purchases ($)	GST (paid; $)	Folio (creditors)
14/06/YY	789	Widgets & Co	550.00	500.00	50.00	Dr CL1

In this example you will notice that we have recorded the payment in the Purchases and GST accounts, and not the Accounts Payable account as previously. We are in fact treating the settlement of our credit purchase as a cash purchase at the time of payment of the account, not at date of invoice or when we received the goods.

The cash payment is then posted to the individual creditor's account to write off the outstanding debt, as shown following:

Creditors Ledger

Creditor's name Widgets & Co **CL1**

Date	Details	Folio	Debit ($)	Credit ($)	Balance ($)
10/06/YY	10 Widgets @ $55	888		550.00	(550.00)
14/06/YY	Paid Account	789	550.00		0.00

Credit sales accounted for on a cash basis under cash accounting

When we make a credit sale, that is, we sell goods with an invoice to be paid sometime in the future, we will update the individual debtor's account with the details of the sale, but we will not include any details of the sale or GST in our accounting records.

Example 5.7 outlines a sale and settlement on credit terms using cash accounting (example 5.3 revisited).

Example 5.7

On 15 June I on-sell the widgets to B Smith at a 50 per cent mark-up using invoice number 987, stipulating that the account is to be settled within 14 days.

In this case, as we are accounting for our sale and GST on a cash basis, we do not enter anything into our accounting records at the time of the actual sale. We will, however, note the sale in our individual debtor's account. The summary of the debtors ledger would normally be reconciled to the Accounts Receivable account; however, in this case, as there is no Accounts Receivable account in our accounting records, the summary total will represent the actual amount that is outstanding to us.

Debtors Ledger

Debtor's name B Smith **DL1**

Date	Details	Invoice	Debit ($)	Credit ($)	Balance ($)
15/06/YY	50 widgets @ $82.50	987	825.00		825.00

On 21 June B Smith sends us a cheque for $825.00

We enter the cheque in settlement of the account in the normal way through the cash receipts journal, but record it in the Sales and GST accounts, as indicated following. We treat the cash settlement as if it were a cash sale.

Cash Receipts Journal **CP1**

Date	Chq #	Particulars	Amount (Bank; $)	Sales ($)	GST (collected; $)	Folio (debtors)
14/06/YY	789	Widgets & Co	550.00	500.00	50.00	Cr D1

Finally, the cash receipt is posted, as totals at the end of the month, to the Cash at Bank, Sales and GST accounts and on an individual basis to the individual debtor's account:

Debtors Ledger

Debtor's name B Smith **DL1**

Date	Details	Invoice	Debit ($)	Credit ($)	Balance ($)
15/06/YY	50 Widgets @ $82.50	987	825.00		825.00
21/06/YY	Cheque received			825.00	0.00

Returns and allowances under cash accounting

If you purchased/sold goods on cash terms, you would simply receive/pay a cash refund processed through the cash receipts and cash payments journals. In the case of credit purchases and sales accounted for under the cash system, there is no record made in the accounts until the amount is settled. Therefore, any allowances and returns are recorded in the individual creditor's or debtor's accounts but not in the accounting system itself. There is no need for the sales returns and purchases returns journals.

In exercise 5.2 we will revisit Mr Jones. This time he is still going to book and pay for a cruise on credit terms, but we are going to account for these transactions under cash accounting rules.

Exercise 5.2

Redo exercise 5.1 as if you were accounting for your credit purchases and credit sales on a cash accounting basis but remember you only update your general ledger Sales, Cash at Bank and GST accounts when the account is actually settled, not when the transactions are entered into. Use the forms drawn up as shown following, with as many lines as you require. A full set of blank forms is available on my website <www.tpabusiness.com.au>.

Debtors Ledger

Debtor's name Mr Jones DL1

Date	Details	Folio	Debit ($)	Credit ($)	Balance ($)

Creditors Ledger

Creditor's name Western Sun Ticketing **CL1**

Date	Details	Folio	Debit ($)	Credit ($)	Balance ($)

Creditors Ledger

Creditor's name City Tours **CL1**

Date	Details	Folio	Debit ($)	Credit ($)	Balance ($)

Cash Receipts Journal CR1

Date	Rec #	Particulars	Amount (Bank; $)	Sales ($)	GST (collected; $)	Folio

Cash Payments Journal CP1

Date	Chq #	Particulars	Amount (Bank; $)	Purchases ($)	GST (paid; $)	Folio

Account name: Purchases **Folio number: 5100**

Date	Details	Folio	Debit ($)	Credit ($)	Balance ($)

Account name: Sales **Folio number: 4100**

Date	Details	Folio	Debit ($)	Credit ($)	Balance ($)

Account name: GST **Folio number: 2900**

Date	Details	Folio	Debit ($)	Credit ($)	Balance ($)

Computerised accounting under cash accounting

As with computerised accounting under the accruals method, we must look at the two types of computerised accounting programs. 'Cash book' accounting programs usually work on a cash basis. You can prepare a quote, convert it into an invoice and when the invoice is paid the relevant general ledger accounts—the Cash at Bank, Sales and GST accounts—are updated.

On the other hand, most computerised 'accounting' programs work under the accruals method. If you wish to create a cash report, they will 'back out' the noncash items, or credit amounts not yet settled, and report the 'cash' position. This means that even if you are using cash accounting, under most computerised 'accounting' systems (as distinct from 'cash book' systems) you will still use the sales and purchases journals, albeit an automated process through the invoice generation and inventory control module.

Some accrual accounting programs also allow you to detach your Purchase and Sales modules and then double-count your cash transactions, once to write off the individual debtor or creditor accounts and again to update the general ledger accounts. This is not really a satisfactory solution.

Revision exercise for day 5

We are a company that purchases essentially the same quantity of goods using credit terms once per month from the one supplier, Mrs Whacko. The goods are to be paid for within 45 days. We commenced purchasing with an order on 1 September that was supplied with an invoice on 15 September. It is now 30 June and our supplier's auditors have asked for a verification of the amount outstanding. Are our records up to the task?

The transactions for the last nine months have been as follows:

15/09/YY	Invoice 1356	$1650
15/10/YY	Invoice 1478	$1320
30/10/YY	Cheque 156	$1650 in settlement of invoice 1356
15/11/YY	Invoice 1498	$1320
30/11/YY	Cheque 157	$1320 in settlement of invoice 1478
15/12/YY	Invoice 1527	$1320
22/12/YY	Adjustment note 67823 of $330 from invoice 1527 (wrong colour)	
23/12/YY	Cheque 158	$1320 in settlement of invoice 1498
15/01/YY	Invoice 1564	$1870
28/01/YY	Cheque 159	$990 in settlement of invoice 1257

15/02/YY	Invoice 1608	$990
01/03/YY	Cheque 160	$1870 in settlement of invoice 1564
15/03/YY	Invoice 1628	$1980
28/03/YY	Cheque 161	$990 in settlement of invoice 1608
28/03/YY	Adjustment note 68945 for $660 for 33.3 per cent promotional discount 1628	
15/04/YY	Invoice 1676	$1320
01/05/YY	Cheque 162	$1320 in settlement of invoice 1628
15/05/YY	Invoice 1801	$1980
30/05/YY	Cheque 163	$1320 in settlement of invoice 1676
15/06/YY	Invoice 1821	$1320
30/06/YY	Cheque 164	$1980 in settlement of invoice 1801

Please enter the 'credit' purchases into Mrs Whacko's individual creditor's account and the payments made into the cash payments journal. Please post the cash payment amounts individually to Mrs Whacko's account and also to the general ledger Purchases and GST accounts.

Creditors Ledger

Creditor's name: Mrs Whacko **CL1**

Date	Details	Folio	Debit ($)	Credit ($)	Balance ($)

Cash Payments Journal **CP1**

Date	Chq #	Particulars	Amount (Bank; $)		Purchases ($)	GST (paid; $)		Folio

Account name: Purchases **Folio number: 5100**

Date	Details	Folio	Debit ($)	Credit ($)	Balance ($)

Account name: GST **Folio number: 2900**

Date	Details	Folio	Debit ($)	Credit ($)	Balance ($)

Day 6

Completing your quarterly BAS

Key terms and concepts

- *Cash accounting:* defined by the Tax Office as a modified cash accounting system where income and expenditure items are accounted for when the cash is received or paid.
- You must never claim a GST credit for private use.

So far we have classified our business transactions through the chart of accounts, recorded them using journals and ledgers, and proved them through a trial balance and bank reconciliation.

However, up until this point we were dealing only with cash transactions. In day 5 those of us who need to account for the purchase and sale of goods made on credit terms were introduced to another set of special journals. These were the Purchases and Sales journals, which are used to record the purchase (and returns) of goods on credit and the sale of those goods on credit. Goods purchased for resale are called inventory items.

We learnt that we must *only* record in these journals goods purchased on credit for resale—inventory items. Please note the two conditions—inventory and credit terms. Your purchase must relate to inventory and not to other credit purchases (such as a motor vehicle), and the purchase must be on credit terms. Inventory purchased or sold for cash is recorded through the cash payments and cash receipts journals respectfully.

Today we will examine the process of completing your quarterly BAS.

Cash accounting revisited

The term 'cash accounting', as it is used in this context, is really a misnomer. What is really meant is that your income and expenses are accounted for when you received or pay the money (as defined by the ATO). Assets and liabilities are still accounted for in the 'normal' manner.

For example, when you purchase inventory on credit terms you account for it—enter the details into your accounting system—only when you actually pay the account. On the other hand, if you were to purchase a motor vehicle or office equipment on credit terms, you would enter the details into your accounts system as an asset purchase and an associated loan, and claim the GST paid in the BAS of that quarter.

This subtle difference is very important when you are calculating your GST liability. You include only the input tax credits (GST paid) and the tax receipts for income and expense items when the account is actually settled, but for asset and liability accounts this occurs when you would normally record the asset or liability in your accounts.

This is outlined in the ATO's fact sheet *Cash and Non-cash Accounting* (NAT 3136), which can be found on the ATO's website <www.ato.gov.au>.

HOW DO I ACCOUNT FOR GST ON A CASH BASIS?

If you are eligible and account for GST on a cash basis you will:

- account for the GST payable on a sale you make in the same tax period you receive payment for the sale. If you receive only part payment for a sale in a tax period, you account only for the part of the GST payment that relates to that part of the sale in that tax period
- claim GST credits for your business purchases in the tax period you pay for them. If you pay only part of the cost of a business purchase in a tax period and have a valid tax invoice, you claim only the GST credit for that part of the cost in that tax period.

You will notice that the statement doesn't refer to business expenses. This is because there is an assumption that all businesses with a turnover under $2 million will pay their expenses in cash when they are due. In other words, you don't enter your invoices received for business expenses into your accounting system until you are required to pay them.

Completing the BAS

Accounting is all about cycles and repetition. Anything that interrupts this cyclic nature will lead to confusions and stress. KIS—keep it simple and do it regularly.

For the purposes of this book I assume that your BAS is required on a quarterly basis and that you lodge a full BAS every quarter. Given that you are now recording your transactions correctly in your accounts and that you are producing a trial balance that contains the correct information, you can now complete your BAS from information contained in that trial balance. You can do this quarterly on a once and for all basis—you work out, report and pay your GST quarterly on the 28th day after the close of each month.

So to complete your BAS, firstly you must finalise your data entry as soon as possible after the last day of each month. It is usual for small businesses to 'do the books' on a given day each week. As soon as possible after the close of each month you will obtain your bank statement and complete your bank reconciliation statement. Given that you can obtain your bank statement electronically, you should be able to complete your monthly accounts and bank reconciliation by the end of the first week after the close of each month. This would be within 14 days after the month's close at the latest.

Since you also do your books on a regular monthly basis, 14 days after each quarter's end you will be in a position to complete your BAS calculation.

The GST is calculated on the previous quarter's transactions, but your trial balance holds the balances of all of your account details for the year. You need to calculate the difference between the two amounts. To do this, if you were completing your December BAS (that is for the months of October, November and December), you would firstly find the trial balance up until the end of the first quarter (to the end of September). Then you would enter the details of that trial balance into a spreadsheet. Now enter the totals for the December trial balance that you have just completed into that spreadsheet. Subtract one from the other and you have the totals for the quarter. This is shown in table 6.1.

Table 6.1: calculating your BAS, step 1—trial balance adjustment

		September Qtr ($)		December Qtr ($)		Difference ($)	
		Dr	Cr	Dr	Cr	Dr	Cr
1100	Cash at Bank	34010		38307		~~4297~~	
1300	Motor vehicles	15423		15423		0	
1400	Office equipment	10876		12566		1690	
2100	Bank loan		30567		25456		~~5111~~
2900	GST		1257		1826		569
3110	Capital		25000		25000	~~0~~	
3120	Drawings	6955		14560		~~7605~~	
3200	Retained earnings		0	0		0	
4100	Sales		80456		190123		109667
5100	Purchases	65891		153449		87558	
6100	Advertising	600		1350		750	
6150	Power	200		400		200	
6170	Interest paid	2125		3950		~~1825~~	
6190	Office rent	1200		2400		1200	
	TOTALS	137280	137280	242405	242405	105125	105125

There are a few things to note about this example:

- The trial balance does not contain debtors, creditors, sales returns and allowances or purchases returns and allowances. This is a trial balance from a cash accounting system.
- The trial balance is entered as both debits and credits. The December BAS Debit column contains GST credit amounts, and the Credit column contains GST collections. Or more strictly speaking, the base amounts from which the input tax credits (ITC) and input tax payable (ITP) amounts can be calculated.
- The Cash at Bank account balance has a line through it. That is because you must first determine which items in your trial balance carry with them a GST credit or a GST liability. Those amounts that do not have an impact on the GST, such as the Cash at Bank account, Bank Loan account, all equity accounts and most importantly the GST account itself, must be deleted from our calculations.
- You will also notice that some amounts are zero. That is because there has been no movement in those accounts for the quarter and therefore no GST impact.

The GST reconciliation

The next step is to work out the GST impact of the trial balance differences. Ignoring all those amounts that do not have a GST impact, you calculate the amount of GST payable by multiplying the difference by 10 per cent. This is shown in table 6.2.

Table 6.2: calculating your BAS, step 2—calculate the GST

		September Qtr ($)		December Qtr ($)		Difference ($)		GST ($)	
		Dr	Cr	Dr	Cr	Dr	Cr		
1100	Cash at Bank	34010		38307		~~4297~~			
1300	Motor vehicles	15423		15423		0			
1400	Office equipment	10876		12566		1690		169	
2100	Bank loan		30567		25456		~~5111~~		
2900	GST		1257		1826		569		
3110	Capital		25000		25000	~~0~~			
3120	Drawings	6955		14560		~~7605~~			
3200	Retained earnings		0	0		0			
4100	Sales		80456		190123		109667		10966
5100	Purchases	65891		153449		87558		8756	
6100	Advertising	600		1350		750		75	
6150	Power	200		400		200		20	
6170	Interest paid	2125		3950		~~1825~~			
6190	Office rent	1200		2400		1200		120	
	TOTALS	137280	137280	242405	242405	105125	105125	9140	10966

So you owe the Tax Office $10 966, from which you may deduct a credit of $9140, making an amount payable of $1826. This amount payable must be equal to the balance of your GST account; if not, you have made a mistake and must start again. This process is known as the 'GST reconciliation'.

Every quarter the Tax Office will send to you a BAS form to be completed and returned. Our job is now to fill in that form, as shown in figure 6.1.

Figure 6.1: BAS GST calculation

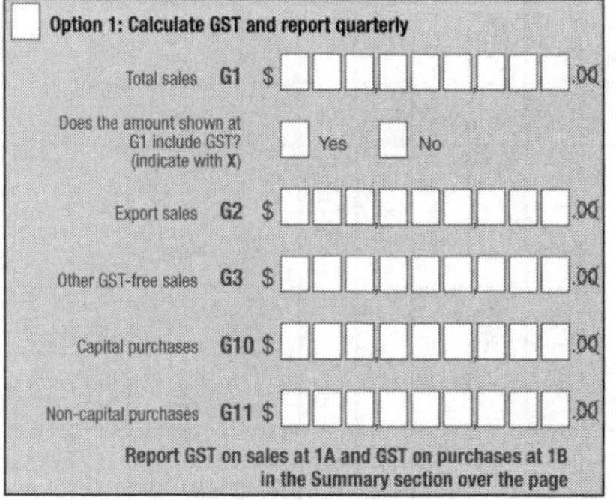

Option 1: Calculate GST and report quarterly

Total sales G1 $ .00

Does the amount shown at G1 include GST? (indicate with X) Yes No

Export sales G2 $ .00

Other GST-free sales G3 $ .00

Capital purchases G10 $ .00

Non-capital purchases G11 $ .00

Report GST on sales at 1A and GST on purchases at 1B in the Summary section over the page

Note

In this example we are going to fill in the BAS directly without using the 'GST Calculation Worksheet for BAS' (see appendix A for a copy of this form). This calculation aid is provided by the ATO to simplify the filling in of your BAS form, but in my opinion it only serves to complicate matters. The completion of the calculation sheet is not mandatory and therefore we are going to ignore it. The reasons for this will be covered later.

We are also going to enter the amounts directly into our BAS form as per the 'differences' column of our trial balance worksheet.

You will notice that the form requires an amount for your 'Total sales', 'Export sales' and 'Other GST-free sales'. For this we need to revist chapter 1, where you completed a chart of accounts for your business. You can see now that if you have any export or GST-free sales, you will have to record these separately from your 'normal' sales. In 99 per cent of cases, small businesses (with the exception of food outlets) do not have export or GST-free sales. If you are a delicatessen owner, for example, your chart of accounts will include Sales and GST-free Sales:

4100 Sales

4200 GST-free Sales

And your cash receipts journal will require an extra column (as shown in table 6.3).

Table 6.3: cash receipts journal form indicating sales and GST-free sales

Cash Receipts Journal **CR1**

Date	Rec #	Particulars	Amount (Bank; $)	Sales ($)	GST-free sales ($)	GST (collected; $)
		TOTALS				
		FOLIO	Dr	Cr	Cr	Cr

Note

For small business owners the Tax Office has set a number of business 'norms' so that you can record all of your sales in one account and then apply a set percentage to those sales to determine the difference between GST and GST-free sales. For example, a cake shop can assume 2 per cent of GST-free sales and a delicatessen can assume 85 per cent. Please refer to the *Simplified GST Accounting Methods for Small Food Retailers* NAT 3185-10.2007.

Armed with this information you can now fill in your BAS referring to the 'differences' section of the worksheet as shown in figure 6.1:

- G1, G2 and G3 come from the Sales section of the trial balance, the total of which equals the total of all of chart of accounts Code 4 Sales: $109 667
- G10 Capital purchases is the total of all GST amounts under chart of accounts Code 1 Assets: $1690
- G11 Non-capital purchases is the total of the chart of accounts Code 5 Cost of sales and Code 6 Expenses: $89 708.

However, there is a catch. The BAS usually requires GST-inclusive data, but as we are using the 'accounts' method you cross the '[No]' box (in answer to the question on the worksheet, 'Does the amount shown at G1 include GST?') and enter the data as calculated, that is, exclusive of the GST. Even though the '[No]' box appears to apply only to 'Total sales', it can in fact apply to all of the data entered when you use the accounts method.

The GST that would normally apply to the total of G1 is then transferred to 1A and the GST for the total of G10 and G11 is then transferred to 1B, as indicated in the summary form in figure 6.2.

1A = 10% of $109 667 = $10 966

1B = 10% of $1690 and $89 708 = $9140

The difference between the GST on the sales of $10967 and the GST on the business inputs of $9140 is $1827, which is the reconciled balance of the GST account rounded to the nearest dollar. When you pay your GST, the GST account will be zeroed off and any amounts entered will make up the balance of the next quarter.

Figure 6.2: GST summary form

Summary

Amounts you owe the Tax Office			Amounts the Tax Office owes you		
GST on sales or GST instalment	1A	$ .00	GST on purchases	1B	$ .00
PAYG tax withheld	4	$ .00	Do not complete 1B if using GST instalment amount (Option 3)		
PAYG income tax instalment	5A	$ .00	Credit from PAYG income tax instalment variation	5B	$ .00
Deferred company/fund instalment	7	$ .00			
1A + 4 + 5A + 7	8A	$ .00	1B + 5B	8B	$ .00

The 'accounts' method of completing the BAS

In this section we have used the accounts method to complete your BAS. This is one of the methods available to you, provided you can readily identify the GST amounts related to your sales, purchases and imports. You must also record separately any purchases or imports that were for input-taxed or GST-free sales. You must also separately record any purchases that were for private use (for details, see 'Private purchases and usage' later in this chapter).

On page 12 of the ATO document *Goods and Services Tax —How to Complete Your Activity Statement* (NAT 7392), the Commissioner states:

> G1 is the only box where you indicate a choice to report GST-exclusive or GST-inclusive amounts. However, if you are using the accounts method you can also complete the other GST boxes as GST-inclusive or GST-exclusive.

I have suggested that we take advantage of this concession and enter all the amounts as GST-exclusive, which is in line with our accounting records.

Amounts without a GST impact

Earlier I stated that you should ignore all those amounts that do not have a GST impact. The most common examples of such amounts are as follows:

- all financial transactions, such as your Cash at Bank account balance and Bank Loan account movements
- financial transactions, such as interest paid or received, and bank fees, mortgage fees or **borrowing costs**
- any movements in your Accounts Payable (Creditors) or Accounts Receivable (Debtors) accounts
- all equity amounts, such as capital, drawings, retained earnings
- all salary and wages, including the PAYG tax amounts and any superannuation deductions
- domestic rents but not commercial rents
- private purchases through your business or the percentage of private use of business assets
- amounts in relation to a motor vehicle in excess of the car limit for the financial year. For example, if your motor car costs in excess of $57 180 for the 2009–10 financial year, you can only claim the GST credit up to the $57 180 limit.

Let's now work through exercise 6.1 to put this into practice.

Exercise 6.1

Carrying on from the above example, we have now come to the March quarter. From the trial balance as shown following, calculate your GST amounts for inclusion in your quarterly BAS.

		March Qtr ($)	
		Dr	Cr
1450	Office computers	3478	
2100	Bank loan		19833
2900	GST		1186
3110	Capital		35000
3120	Drawings	21138	
3200	Retained earnings		0
4100	Sales		285796
5100	Purchases	231872	
6100	Advertising	1850	
6150	Power	600	
6170	Interest paid	5595	
6190	Office rent	3600	
	TOTALS	341815	341815

Required:

G1 Total sales
G10 Capital purchases
G11 Non-capital purchases
1A GST on sales
1B GST on purchases

Difference = GST payable. Does it reconcile with your GST account?

Using the GST calculation worksheet for BAS

I have suggested that we avoid using the 'GST Calculation Worksheet for BAS' (see appendix A for a copy of this form) for a number of reasons but mainly because it doesn't allow for amounts net of the GST to be entered directly from your trial balance. You must instead add the GST component to these amounts in order to calculate the GST as one-eleventh of the final amount at the end of the process. This is not only a tedious process but prone to error.

You will also notice that the amounts entered into the calculation sheet are just duplicates of the BAS amounts. There appears to be no real reason to complete this process twice.

GST adjustments

There are three types of GST adjustments. Firstly, there are the adjustments that occur through normal business activity, such as receiving a discount for a GST purchase after the purchase has been completed. For example, you purchase goods on credit and are allowed a discount for early payment. Other business adjustments can occur when goods are returned or an allowance made. All of these adjustments are netted off against your sales amount and appear as one net figure at G1 in your BAS. This is especially relevant to small businesses that use cash accounting.

The second type of adjustment is for the personal use of an asset, or goods used for private use (for more information, see 'Private purchases and usage' in the following section).

The third type of adjustment is to allow for a mistake. Let's assume that you should have entered $10 950 at G1 in your BAS but instead you entered $20 950. For this type of error we need to adjust our BAS. If the mistake was made less than 18 months ago and the total adjustment is less than $5000, you can simply make the adjustment on your next BAS (for details, see the ATO document *Correcting GST Mistakes*). But you cannot use this as a tax manipulation tool—you can only correct mistakes that are genuine and reasonable. For mistakes over $5000 or that occurred over 18 months ago, first refer to the ATO document *Correcting GST Mistakes* and then contact the ATO. See appendix A for more information on the ATO's fact sheets.

Private purchases and usage

Small business owners often find it more cost effective to purchase certain household items through their business. There is absolutely nothing wrong with doing this but you must ensure that you treat such purchases as strictly private—that is, you must record the payment as a drawing (or allocate to the Private Use equity account) and not as an inventory purchase or an asset acquisition and you must not allocate any of the GST components to the GST account. You cannot claim any GST credits for private purchases.

If you take **trading stock** for your own use, then again you must journal out the value of trading stock from your purchases and also adjust your GST account.

Private usage of business assets is the other form of private use. Let's use the example of a home-based business that buys a business computer that will also be used by the household for private use. In this case you must estimate the private-use percentage and only record the business portion of the purchase in your records. The easiest method is to note on the invoice your private-use percentage and then, when you record the payment in your cash book, allocate the private amount to an equity account, such as Capital (reduction; we assume a sole trader in this book), Drawings or Private Use, and split the business portion between the asset and GST accounts. You cannot claim the GST credit for the private-use portion.

Let's work through example 6.2 to see how this works.

Example 6.2

Assume that we purchase a computer for $3300 of which a third is considered to be for private use. The cash payments journal entry could look like the following:

Cash Payments Journal **CP1**

Date	Particulars	Amount (Bank; $)	GST (paid; $)	Other payments	
				Amount ($)	Details
01/05/YY	PC Computers	3300.00	200.00	2000.00	Office equipment
				1100.00	Private use

The use of the equity account called 'Private Use' to allocate the $1100.00 will provide external users of your accounts (your accountant, or the GST and income tax auditors) with a more-detailed explanation of your actions.

Motor vehicles

When you purchase a motor vehicle you create an asset account for that vehicle and add to it your business portion of the purchase price, net of the GST component. If the vehicle is a 100 per cent work vehicle, such as a van, the full purchase price is added to the Motor Vehicle account. If it is a motor vehicle that is also used for family purposes, only the portion that relates to business use is added to the Motor Vehicle account. This is the same as we discussed for a computer also used by the household for private use; however, if the car is a family vehicle, there is a limit to the amount you can claim. This limit is referred to as the luxury car tax threshold. (The car limit for the 2009–10 financial year was $57 180.)

In order to determine the business-use percentage, you usually keep a diary for six weeks and base your estimate upon that figure.

However, the ownership of a motor vehicle also includes expenses, such as registration, insurance, fuel and servicing. All of these expenses will be added to your Motor Vehicle Expenses account but the amount added will again only be the business-use portion, net of any GST credits, as determined by your business-use percentage. Your private-use portion along with the private-use GST credits will be debited to an equity account, such as Drawings, or a Personal Use account.

You must never claim any GST credit for the private-use portion of motor vehicle expenses.

You must also ensure that you can clearly identify your motor vehicle expenses on a vehicle by vehicle basis, as the calculation of your income tax involves a deduction for your motor vehicle expenses that may be based upon a formula rather than the actual expenses themselves.

If you lease a vehicle, the same rules apply in regard to the private-use component; however, in this case you don't create an asset account since the lease payment itself is an expense and you cannot claim both the GST on the purchase of the vehicle and the GST on the lease payments. It is one or the other. For more information on leasing, see the ATO document *Hire Purchase, Leasing and the GST*.

For more information on the GST and motor vehicles, see the ATO document *GST and Motor Vehicles*. See also appendix A for more information on the ATO's fact sheets.

Note

The purchase of a dual-use motor vehicle for a sole proprietor can be treated as previously described under motor vehicles but in all other instances it can also trigger fringe benefits tax problems. There are also four different methods of calculating the income tax deductions for motor vehicles used in small business. It would be prudent to consult your accountant before you record your purchase of such a vehicle in your books.

Computerised accounting

Most computerised accounting programs will automate the production of your BAS. Usually this is in the form of a worksheet from which you can transfer your information onto your BAS form itself. Problems occur when the program produces figures that don't make sense, such as a negative capital purchase, and you are the one who has to fix it. In short, you must know how to manually complete your BAS in order to effectively use a computerised accounting system.

If you refer to a standard small business chart of accounts, you will see the GST and BAS codes that have been allocated to each chart of accounts item. I hope that by doing the previous BAS exercise these codes now make more sense to you. The BAS codes are taken from the BAS form itself, but the GST codes used in this example are unique to the accounting package (each accounting program will have its own GST codes, although they all tend to be similar). Table 6.4 shows examples of common GST codes.

Table 6.4: example of GST codes that could be used in an accounting package

GST codes	Description	GST codes	Description
GST	GST included in cost	FBT	Fringe benefits tax
NT	Nonreportable	WT	Withholding tax
INP	Input taxed amount	PER	Personal use
SAL	Salary and wages	FRE	GST free
PYE	PAYE deductions		

Most computerised accounting programs require that you allocate a 'default' GST code to each account. This can then be modified on data input if required. The GST code along with the account type (such as asset or liability) is used by the BAS preparation module in creating the BAS report.

Computerised accounting and private-use calculations

No computerised accounting program that I am aware of automates private-use calculations. This is a manual calculation that is entered into your accounting system no matter whether you are using a manual system or a 'cash book' program for full computerised accounting.

Revision exercise for day 6

For the June quarter I made the following business transactions:

- I paid $1186 to the Tax Office for GST outstanding.
- I purchased a new office computer for $3300 (including GST) of which a third is considered to be for private use.
- I paid $5600 off my bank loan.
- I withdrew $5500 for private use.
- I made $82 940 in sales.
- I purchased $62 150 of goods.
- I spent $429 on advertising.
- I paid $220 for electricity.
- I paid $1037 in interest charges.
- I paid $1320 on office rent.

Required:

G1	Total sales
G10	Capital purchases
G11	Non-capital purchases
1A	GST on sales
1B	GST on purchases

Difference = GST payable. Does it reconcile with your GST account?

Day 7

Some special rules for small business

Key terms and concepts

- *Turnover:* your gross income from all of your business activities before any deductions have been made.
- A business is a small business if its turnover is less than $2 million per year.
- An expense is something that is consumed or classified as expenditure on a asset costing less than $1000.
- A repair can only be an expense if it does not improve the asset.

So far we have classified our business transactions through our chart of accounts, recorded them in journals and summarised them into general ledger accounts. After proving the bank accounts using the bank reconciliation process we produced a trial balance and from there completed the BAS.

Our next challenge is to examine the special rules, often referred to as the Small Business Tax Concessions, that govern the bookkeeping process for small businesses. For the purposes of this book, we will refer only to those concessions that have an impact on bookkeeping rather than accounting.

Eligibility for small businesses

The ATO allows small business owners to report both their GST liability and their income tax on a cash basis provided that their annual turnover is under $2 million. There are a number of other taxation concessions provided to small business owners, a few of which we will examine throughout this chapter, in particular, those that pertain to the bookkeeping of your accounts.

Turnover includes all ordinary income you earn in the ordinary course of business for the income year. You can use your actual figures from this year or last year, or you can estimate your turnover after taking all relevant circumstances into account. In practice, ongoing businesses base this year's estimated turnover on their latest set of figures, provided that there is no real reason to believe that they will be substantially different for this period.

Turnover means your gross income, not your net profit. It includes such items as your gross sales, fees, income and bank interest received, but does not include any GST amount. It is also an aggregate turnover, that is, it includes turnover from all the business activities that you are associated with.

The amounts not included in your turnover are those that you receive outside your normal trading activity, such as the profit made on the disposal of assets or loan monies received.

Provided that your annual turnover is under $2 million you can access the special taxation concessions available to small business working within the micro market, often called micro businesses.

When is an outlay an expense and when is it an asset?

Technically, any expenditure that is likely to provide a business benefit for future years is an asset. An expenditure that only provides a benefit to the current year is an expense. So, if I buy a fountain pen for $60 that is going to last for five years or more, is it an asset?

The answer is technically yes, but the Tax Office has made a special concession for small businesses whereby if you have a total outlay on a good that is less than $1000, you can classify that outlay as an expense irrespective of whether or not it may technically be an asset. This is one of the most useful taxation concessions and it means that a lot of unnecessary recording of assets of minor value can be avoided. However, it is also the most abused.

When deciding whether or not an outlay is an expense or an asset, you must look at the total expenditure. A computer system would be an asset if all of the components in total add up to over $1000 even if each individual part, such as the CPU, the monitor and keyboard, are under $1000.

And further, just because an outlay is over $1000 does not of itself make the outlay an asset. A $1200 electricity bill is still an expense, as the electricity purchased was consumed in this financial year and is of no future ongoing benefit to the business. It is the combination of a future benefit and a total outlay in excess of $1000 that defines an outlay as an asset.

Depreciation

From the very first time that we start to use any asset, with the exception of land, the value of that asset will start to depreciate—in tax speak, **decline in value**. Each year we estimate the decline in value of our assets and create an expense account called Depreciation to account for this. In the end, the total value of our asset purchases will end up as an expense.

This process of estimation of the value of **depreciation** and creation of the Depreciation expense accounts is a matter for your accountant as part of your end-of-year income tax calculations and reporting process and is beyond the scope of this book.

Assets and record keeping

It is most important that every asset you purchase has its own file made up to contain all of the information that relates to that asset, such as original purchase agreements, registration and insurance documents, details of any improvements made and evidence of how you determined the private use percentage. The main reason for making such a file is that your accountant will need all of this information when you come to dispose of the asset.

Every year you will also have to inform your accountant of all of your asset purchases and disposals throughout the year, plus any improvements you have made to your existing assets. This will allow your accountant to update your assets register for depreciation purposes. This is usually held in the form of a spreadsheet and you should either update it annually yourself, or if this is done by your accountant, you should be provided with an updated copy for your records.

Repair or improvement?

As an asset wears out it will need to be repaired or enhanced. How do we treat this additional expenditure?

If we are adding to, or improving an asset, the value of that improvement is added to the value of the asset (in tax speak, a second element cost). The depreciation expense for that asset is then adjusted to take into account the improvement. For example, we purchase a 4WD vehicle for $40 000. Shortly afterwards we purchase a bull bar for $1200. The value of the bull bar is added to the original vehicle purchase amount and we now have a vehicle worth $41 200. And the cost of the addition plays no part in determining the classification of the outlay. The purchase of a winch for the vehicle for $500 will still be added to the asset (the vehicle) irrespective of the fact that this outlay is under $1000, as the 'total' asset value is over $1000 and additional outlays that improve the asset are added to the asset's cost (in tax speak, its cost base).

However, if the outlay is for a repair, then the amount is classified as an expense. Using the 4WD example just discussed, all the standard servicing and repairs to the vehicle to bring it back to its 'original' state are classified as expenses. For example, the radiator develops a leak. The repair and replacement of that radiator is an expense of running the vehicle, just like adding petrol to the tank or replacing new tyres when the original ones wear out.

And now for the murky areas. Tax problems rarely involve the straightforward; they are usually fought on the in-between ground. Let's use the previous example of the 4WD's radiator and imagine that the radiator blew up because it wasn't suited to the driving conditions the vehicle was being subjected to. When we replaced the radiator we didn't just replace like for like but rather we installed a newer bigger and better replacement. In this case that would constitute an improvement to the asset and the whole amount of the repair would be included in the asset's cost base. It's not possible to expense an amount equivalent to what the radiator would have cost if a similar one had been installed and just add the difference to the asset's cost base. It's all or nothing.

And an even murkier situation arises if you had intended to replace your old radiator with the same model and it was no longer available and you had to accept an upgraded model. Provided that it really was your intention to replace like for like, an improvement in these situations can still be treated as an expense. The 'reasonableness' test must always be applied in these circumstances as such problems often occur with technology, especially computer repairs.

Spare parts

The acquisition of spare parts can be treated in a number of ways depending upon their intended use. If they are being held for resale, for use in the repair of customer's equipment or in the manufacture of new items, then they are held as inventory. Examples are a hard drive held by a computer shop or engine parts held by a garage.

If they are being held for the repair of your own equipment, they are to be classified as an asset called 'Spare parts held in reserve'. As they are acting as spare parts (that is, they will not be installed ready for use but rather they will be held in reserve), they are not included in the asset's cost base or reclassified as an expense until they are used.

If the spare parts are used for the repair of your equipment, the repairing of which only restores the machine to its original state, then they are reclassified as a repair expense at that point. If, on the other hand, the 'repair' enhances the original state, then the cost of the spare part is added to the original asset cost and depreciated accordingly. However, if you replace a damaged part with a better one, simply because of the advancement in technology, it is still just a repair.

When you dispose of the old worn-out equipment, any money received is classified as miscellaneous income, but don't forget the GST component.

Another type of spare part is the 'rotating spare part'. An example of this is a racing car with three engines that are constantly being 'rotated' through the car. In this instance the 'spare parts' are assets that are installed (in turn) and therefore are subject to depreciation just like any other depreciating asset. If the spares are 'attached' to the same unit, then the whole unit, including the spares, is the depreciable asset and the spare part is a second element cost of that asset. If the spares are 'pooled', then each spare part, for example, each engine, is a separate asset.

If you purchase spare parts for mixed purposes (that is, they could be used for both your own equipment or for resale, repair or manufacture), then they would be classified as trading stock. If you use the stock for your own purposes, the time you transfer it out of trading stock is when you reclassify it as either a depreciable asset or a repair expense as the situation requires.

Note

The term 'reclassify' as used in this context in bookkeeping terms would translate into a journal entry. You would credit the Spare Parts Held in Reserve account with the cost (net of GST) of the spare part and debit either the asset into which it has been installed or a repair and maintenance expense account as the circumstances dictate. But don't forget to advise your accountant of your actions at the end of the financial year so that they can review your work to ensure that it fully complies with the tax law as it applies at the time.

Replacement tools

It would not be unusual for a set of tradesman's quality tools to cost in excess of $1000. If you purchase the tools as a one-off item, you would classify the initial purchase as an asset. Whenever you add a 'new' tool to the set, that addition would also be an asset. It would, in tax terms, be a second element cost. However, if you purchase a replacement tool for one that is broken, past its useful life or lost, then that outlay would be an expense.

The same concept can be applied in a number of situations; the purchase of linen for a hotel is another classic example.

Consumables

Consumable items, such as oils, rags and welding rods, are usually an expense unless they are held for sale as trading stock, in which case they are treated just like any other item of trading stock.

Prepaid expenses

When you pay your annual insurance on your motor vehicle you are actually paying the account in advance, effectively a prepaid expense. Examples of some other common prepaid expenses are professional association fees, software support fees, council rates, water rates and even your telephone or PABX rental. You would classify all such outlays as an expense at the time you actually made the payment.

However, for income tax purposes the situation is a little different. The tax law has special rules in regard to prepayments.

As a small business taxpayer, if the payment is for less than $1000 or is in the nature of wages or a salary, or the payment is by court order, then your accountant can continue to claim it as an outright expense.

If a prepayment expense does not fit into these categories, as a small business you can continue to claim these expenses outright, provided that you do not prepay more than 12 months in advance and the period your prepayment covers ends no later than the end of the next financial year. However, in the unlikely event that the prepayment covers a period in excess of 12 months and is greater than $1000, you must advise your accountant of that situation so that, for income tax purposes, the expense can be proportioned over the financial years concerned.

Accounting for credit card purchases

Firstly, you should create a credit card liability account to hold your credit card purchases, such as the following example:

4350 Commonwealth Visa

When you make a purchase using your credit card you are considered to have made a cash purchase at that time; however, it would be a waste of time to attempt to enter into your system each and every individual credit card purchase. There are some instances where you may wish to do this, though, especially for large purchases of inventory items for a special job (in tax speak, job costing).

Credit cards usually have an extended payment period, say 60 days from the date of purchase, so that when you receive your credit card statement you usually don't have to pay it immediately. So the first step is to 'code' your statement, that is, to allocate a chart of account number to each item purchased. For example, you may have four items that relate to the purchase of petrol for your work van. You would code all of these under the same account number. You should also be aware of any private purchases or amounts that have a private component.

Now that you have all of your items coded, you add together all those of the same account code in order to get the one amount per code that you will enter into your system. The total of all of your account-coded amounts should equal the total of your statement amount. If your statement crosses over the month's end, you may wish to split your statement in two, one part that covers this month and the second part covering next month, and code each part separately. You must do this if the month's end is also the end of that financial quarter for GST purposes.

You can now enter the credit card statement into your system as a cash payment, against the credit card liability account rather than your day-to-day bank accounts. Don't forget the GST component and especially do not claim the GST component on any private purchases. Private purchases should be applied to the Drawings or Private Use equity account in full without any deduction for the GST. You would use the statement date as the date of entry, unless you split the statement for GST purposes, in which case you enter one amount at the month's end and the remainder at the statement date.

When it comes time to pay your credit card, you enter another cash payment, this time as a No GST amount credited against (reducing) your Cash at Bank account and debited against (reducing) your GST liability account.

You should note that the above process is completely in accord with the ATO'S ruling on GST and credit cards, even when you are using a cash-based method of accounting, which states (emphasis added):

> Goods and services tax ruling GSTR 2003/12 'Goods and services tax: when consideration is provided and received for various payment instruments and other methods of payment'
>
> **Where you account on the cash basis**
>
> 19. Subsection 29-10(2) attributes the input tax credit to which *you are entitled for a creditable acquisition to the tax period in which you provide consideration*, but only to the extent that you provided the consideration in that tax period.
>
> **Credit card**
>
> 30. When a payment is made by credit card in person, *consideration is provided and received when the recipient of the supply signs the docket to authorise the transaction.* When a payment is made remotely (for example, by telephone or through the Internet), the consideration is provided and received when the cardholder gives the card number and other required details.

Accounting for loan repayments

Business loans are usually in the form of either a bank **overdraft** or a business loan. The fees and interest you pay on these loans are expenses, whereas the principal repayment is offset against the original liability.

If you are using a bank overdraft facility, you account for the fees and interest as part of the bank reconciliation process. An overdraft is just like any other bank account, but with a negative rather than a positive balance. When you draw funds out of your bank overdraft those funds are not income for your business but rather a liability, albeit accounted for as a negative Bank account asset. It is the interest and fees on that overdraft that is transferred each month into an expense account.

If you have a business loan, the accounting is a little more complex. When you receive money, say a cheque of $100 000, you bank the cheque in your normal operating account and create a liability account to hold the outstanding balance, as shown following:

Debit Bank account (asset)	100 000	
Credit Loan account (liability)		100 000

When a repayment is made, the interest component is an expense and only the principal repayment is deducted from the liability account. However, it is normally not practical to distinguish what is what for each repayment and therefore the repayments are normally offset directly against the liability account:

Dr Loan account (liability)	3000	
Cr Bank account		3000

At the end of each quarter you are then required to determine the amount of principal repaid and what's left is interest and fees. Let's assume that you received the loan on 1 July and made three $3000 monthly repayments. It is now 30 September and your Loan account should appear as shown in table 7.1.

Table 7.1: Loan account as at 30 September YY

Date	Particulars	Debit ($)	Credit ($)	Balance ($)
01/7/YY	Business loan received		100 000	(100 000)
30/7/YY	July repayment	3 000		(97 000)
30/8/YY	August repayment	3 000		(94 000)
30/9/YY	September repayment	3 000		(91 000)

On 30 September you ring the finance company and determine that the outstanding balance (after your 30 September payment) is actually $95 000. Comparing this with the account balance, you can see that the fees and interest amount to $4000 for the period. You now journal this amount into the expense account, as shown:

Dr Interest Expense account (asset)	4000	
Cr Loan account (liability)		4000

The Interest Expense account now contains the fees expense and the Loan account now reflects the correct balance, as shown in table 7.2.

Table 7.2: Loan account reflecting correct balance

Date	Particulars	Debit ($)	Credit ($)	Balance ($)
01/7/YY	Business loan received		100 000	(100 000)
30/7/YY	July repayment	3 000		(97 000)
30/8/YY	August repayment	3 000		(94 000)
30/9/YY	September repayment	3 000		(91 000)
30/9/YY	Quarterly interest		4 000	(95 000)

Leased and hire purchase assets

The term 'lease' can have different outcomes depending on whether it is an operating lease or a financial lease. An operating lease is what we call a rental agreement. A financial lease is what we would call a purchase. If we rent premises by a lease, this is an operating lease; if we buy a car by lease, where we will own it at the end of the period, this is a financial arrangement.

If we have a rental (operating) lease, each lease payment is an expense and the GST (as indicated on the rent invoice) is creditable in full (subject to the private use issue discussed previously). However, you do not get any GST credit when you first start to hold the asset, nor is there any depreciation available. If you account for the GST on a cash basis, then you can claim the GST credit when you actually make the lease payment rather than when the payment is due.

As the GST requires that a lease is treated as a 'rental' and because the difference between the two methods of accounting, depreciation and interest versus lease payment expense, is only marginal, most small businesses treat all leases as rental arrangements. You do not record the asset purchase in your books but rather you treat the lease payments as expenses and claim the GST credit accordingly.

However, you can only expense that portion of the lease payment that relates to business use. You would need to split the payment between private use that is applied to an equity account in full and the business use that is split between the GST component and the expense amount. If you make no allowance for the private use of assets, you are liable to be caught in the FBT trap.

Note

With regard to leased motor vehicles, ask your accountant about treating the whole lease payment as an expense and using the generous fringe benefits tax motor vehicle concessions to account for the private use. The actual fringe benefits tax can be avoided by a private contribution, accounted for through your Drawings account.

Home office tax traps

The home office can be a tax nightmare for the unwary.

Based on the ATO document *Home-based Business*, there are two scenarios that you should be aware of. Firstly, you run your business elsewhere and only have a home office for after hours work (called a home work area) or, secondly, you have set aside a specific area of your home to run a home-based business from. See appendix A for details about this document and other fact sheets provided by the ATO.

If you have a home work area and your main business is located elsewhere, you can claim the running expenses of the home office to the extent that they are business related. According to the ATO document, these expenses could include:

- the cost of using a room's utilities, such as gas, water and electricity
- business phone and internet costs
- depreciation of office plant and equipment (for example, desks, chairs, computers, curtains, carpets and light fittings).

However, if you are actually running the business from home and you have allocated an area to the business, then in addition to the expenses we've listed you can also claim the 'occupancy' costs, such as interest on your mortgage (based on the percentage of your home used for your business).

The main problem with claiming the running expenses of your home office on tax is that when you come to sell your home, you will have to pay tax on the 'business' percentage of capital gains made in the sale. Effectively, your home is only partially exempt from capital gains when used for business purposes. According to the ATO, you may even have to pay capital gains if you:

- do not actually claim deductions for occupancy or running expenses
- have never claimed a deduction for any interest on money you borrowed to buy your home
- owned your home outright before you started using any part of it to produce income
- have started a business from home but have not yet made a profit.

The message is clear—talk to your accountant before setting aside any part of your home for business purposes!

When does my hobby become a business?

A hobby is something you do for enjoyment, whereas a business is something that you do for profit.

The main taxation difference is that hobbies that earn an income that is incidental to their main purpose of enjoyment are not subject to tax on that income. You do not register for an ABN and you do not complete a BAS and you cannot issue tax invoices. Therefore you cannot claim any GST credits on your hobby inputs nor do you add GST to any sales that you make. You are in GST terms input taxed and in income tax terms your income is nonassessable nonexempt (NANE income).

However, if you are in business, you must register for an ABN and your income is assessable. You can issue tax invoices and if you are registered for the GST, you add GST to your sales and claim a GST credit for your business inputs. You also must complete a quarterly BAS (as a micro business).

So, provided that your 'hobby' earns less than $75 000 (the upper limit where you have to register for the GST) and makes an overall tax loss, or if you consider yourself to be in business and you make an overall tax profit, then the Tax Office is unlikely to query your assumption. However, if your hobby makes a profit or has a turnover in excess of $75 000, then you will need to justify your position. Likewise, if your 'business' makes a loss and you wish to claim this loss against your other assessable income, you will also most likely be requested to justify your position.

The GST legislation has made the business/hobby distinction a little clearer. If you earn over $75 000, you must register for the GST. To do this you must obtain an ABN, which by definition means that you are in business. In practical terms, there are very few 'hobbies' that earn over $75 000 per annum.

The other GST complication is the tax invoice. Hobbies cannot issue a tax invoice because you do not have an ABN. However, if you sell your product to another 'business', that is , someone registered for the GST, then your client will be obliged to withhold 48.5 per cent of the invoice price and remit this to the Tax Office as a 'withholding' amount. They will also be unable to claim any GST amount on the purchases. Therefore 'hobbies' are effectively precluded for making any 'business' sales. You can sell to the public in general, for example, through a market stall, but you cannot make a sale to an ABN registered entity. As an example you could not sell your wares to a business owner who ran a market stall in order that they could on-sell to the public at large.

The upshot is that if you start a hobby and then decide to sell your product to the public in general, provided that you do not make a 'profit' from your enterprise, it can still be considered a hobby. You could, for example, make wooden toys in your back shed and sell them to the public at a market stall in order to offset costs, and this exercise would still be considered to be a hobby. However, once you start to make a taxable profit from this enterprise, or it starts to take on the look and feel of a business, then you should seek professional advice in regard to your particular situation.

The ATO has issued some guidelines on this topic that your accountant will need to consider. They are as follows:

- Does your activity appear to be commercial in nature?
- Are you really in business, or are you still just planning and evaluating your idea for a business?
- Is your intention to make a profit in the long term?
- Is your activity a 'one-off' transaction, or a regular activity? 'One-off' transactions are usually not classified as a business.
- Is the way you operate consistent with industry norms or other businesses in your industry?
- How big is your activity? Is its size or scale sufficient to allow you to make a sustainable profit?
- Do you have a plan, or are you just flying by the seat of your pants? To check the answer to this, ask yourself

whether you can produce business records and books of account, a separate business bank account, business premises, licences or qualifications and a registered business name.

Where to from here?

Throughout this book we have looked at setting up a manual accounting system from the creation of the chart of accounts through to the recording of our business transactions and taking them to the trial balance stage. Our final task was to complete the BAS.

However, that is not the end of the story. At the end of the financial year you must produce your financial reports, the profit and loss statement (also known as an income statement) and the balance sheet. It is from the profit and loss statement that you derive your taxable income upon which you pay your income tax.

The process of adjusting the trial balance figures so that they can be used for reporting purposes is called accounting. This entails matching your expenses with your income, determining the non-cash items, such as depreciation, and correctly recording your closing inventory. Under the Tax Office rules all of these adjustments are subject to special concessions aimed at making the process easier, but all of that is for another day.

How does my accountant fit into all of this?

Your accountant has three vital roles to play in your business.

The first role is in relation to your taxation. This can take the form of a review of your GST liability, the calculation of your annual income tax liability and in some cases a review of your fringe benefits tax liability. To do this they will need access to your complete set of books at the end of the financial year, after you have completed your final bank reconciliation and BAS. In manual systems this would consist of a complete photocopy of all journals and accounts, and in a computerised system, a complete backup disk of the year's work. You must also provide full details of all asset purchases and sales during the year, any abnormal transactions and any expenses that you have paid that will have an effect for over one year, such as insurance premiums that are more than just an annual renewal.

Your accountant will then undertake the end-of-year process and advise you how to complete your books and roll over into the new year. This is the accounting function.

The second role your accountant plays is as your first line of defence. They are the person you contact if you have any problems. I hope this book has explained the bookkeeping function to the extent that you won't need to ask your accountant many day-to-day questions and you can resolve any issues yourself, keeping in mind that accountants charge by the six-minute unit. A junior member of the firm will cost about $200 per hour and it will cost up to $600 or more for a partner's time. It can cost up to $25 just to readdress a letter to you.

A few tips: demand that a copy of all of your accountant's working papers are provided to you at the end of their annual tax review. You paid for them, so you deserve to have them. Make sure the papers include a depreciation schedule. Also demand that the 'Address for Service' is your own premises and not your accountant's office. A simple Tax Office flyer could cost you $25 in redirection fees.

And finally, your accountant should be in a position to advise you on the best ways to expand your business and assist you with cash flow statements, budgeting and loan applications. But again, all of this is at a cost, those dreaded six-minute units!

Computerised accounting—a final postscript

I hope that this book has given you a good understanding of the manual accounting process involved in bookkeeping. I cannot stress enough how important it is that you fully understand this process before you attempt to understand the complexities of a computerised accounting package, albeit a 'cash book' or a full accounting program.

Appendix A
Useful resources

Author's website

On my website <www.tpabusiness.com.au>, under 'Learn Bookkeeping in 7 Days', you will find a full set of blank accounting forms as well as blank 'exercise' forms for the revision exercises from day 2 through to day 6.

In addition, I will provide additional resources as time permits. Please check the website for the latest updates. If you are a reader, student or lecturer and wish to share examples, overheads and other material with the general community, please email me at <rod@tpabusiness.com.au> and I will consider them for inclusion in the resources.

Australian Taxation Office fact sheets

The following fact sheets are available from the ATO website <www.ato.gov.au>. Just type the relevant 'NAT' number indicated into the search box to go straight to the publication you wish to access. Some of these fact sheets can be downloaded as PDF files and others can only be read onscreen or printed for your reference:

- *Cash and Non-cash Accounting* (NAT 3136)
- *Correcting GST Mistakes* (NAT 4700)
- *Goods and Services Tax—How to Complete Your Activity Statement* (NAT 7392)
- *GST and Motor Vehicles* (NAT 4629)
- *GST for Small Business* (NAT 3014)
- *Home-based Business* (NAT 10709)
- *Tax Basics for Small Business* (NAT 1908).

Computerised accounting packages

Demonstration versions of computerised accounting packages are available for both a full accounting program and cash book accounting:

- Full accounting program: 'MYOB Accounting' by MYOB Technology Pty Ltd; <www.myob.com.au>.
- Cash book accounting: 'Cashbook Complete' by Acclaim Software Ltd; <www.acclaimsoftware.com.au>.

Books

The following For Dummies books may be useful:

- *Bookkeeping For Dummies* by Veechi Curtis and Lynley Averis, Wiley, 2010.

This brand-new book has been completely rewritten from the original US edition to reflect Australian conditions. It applies to all small businesses but is especially focused on the SME enterprises with over $2 million in turnover and using accrual accounting in accordance with Australian accounting standards. This contrasts with *Learn Bookkeeping in 7 Days,* which is aimed at micro businesses earning less than $2 million per year and using cash accounting methods as outlined by the ATO.

- *Tax for Australians For Dummies* by Jimmy B Prince, Wiley, 2009.

  This book explains Australian taxation in simple terms. Its author, Jimmy B Prince, is a former lecturer in income tax law at La Trobe University. It has been technically reviewed by the CPA Australia senior tax counsel and therefore has the tick of approval of Australia's leading accounting association.

- *DIY Super For Dummies* by Trish Power, Wiley, 2009.

  Superannuation, especially DIY super, is a minefield for the unwary. If you are contemplating setting up your own super fund, this book is a must. Its author, Trish Power, is a highly respected writer of 10 books on the subject. It has been technically reviewed by Mark Morris in the CPA December issue of *InTheBlack,* and therefore comes highly recommended by Australia's leading accounting association.

GST calculation worksheet

Below is the GST calculation worksheet that you can use to help you calculate your BAS.

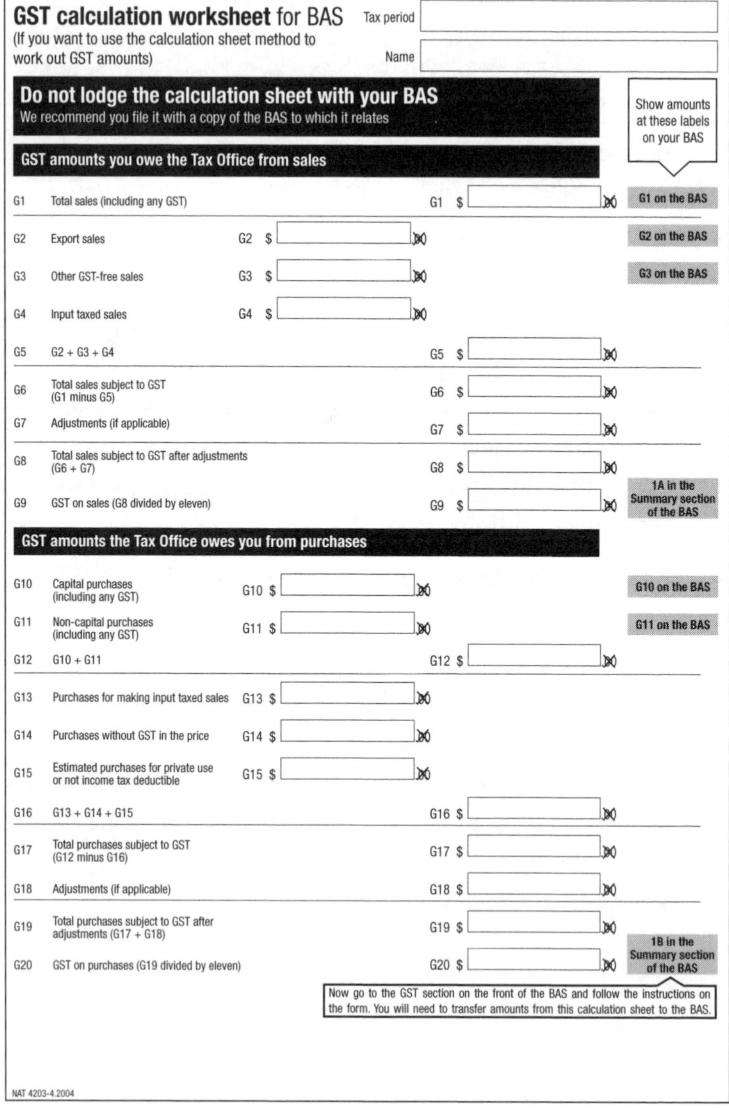

GST calculation worksheet for BAS

Tax period

(If you want to use the calculation sheet method to work out GST amounts)

Name

Do not lodge the calculation sheet with your BAS

We recommend you file it with a copy of the BAS to which it relates

Show amounts at these labels on your BAS

GST amounts you owe the Tax Office from sales

				Show amounts at these labels on your BAS
G1	Total sales (including any GST)		G1 $ .00	G1 on the BAS
G2	Export sales	G2 $ .00		G2 on the BAS
G3	Other GST-free sales	G3 $ .00		G3 on the BAS
G4	Input taxed sales	G4 $ .00		
G5	G2 + G3 + G4		G5 $ .00	
G6	Total sales subject to GST (G1 minus G5)		G6 $ .00	
G7	Adjustments (if applicable)		G7 $ .00	
G8	Total sales subject to GST after adjustments (G6 + G7)		G8 $ .00	
G9	GST on sales (G8 divided by eleven)		G9 $ .00	1A in the Summary section of the BAS

GST amounts the Tax Office owes you from purchases

G10	Capital purchases (including any GST)	G10 $ .00		G10 on the BAS
G11	Non-capital purchases (including any GST)	G11 $ .00		G11 on the BAS
G12	G10 + G11		G12 $ .00	
G13	Purchases for making input taxed sales	G13 $ .00		
G14	Purchases without GST in the price	G14 $ .00		
G15	Estimated purchases for private use or not income tax deductible	G15 $ .00		
G16	G13 + G14 + G15		G16 $ .00	
G17	Total purchases subject to GST (G12 minus G16)		G17 $ .00	
G18	Adjustments (if applicable)		G18 $ .00	
G19	Total purchases subject to GST after adjustments (G17 + G18)		G19 $ .00	
G20	GST on purchases (G19 divided by eleven)		G20 $ .00	1B in the Summary section of the BAS

Now go to the GST section on the front of the BAS and follow the instructions on the form. You will need to transfer amounts from this calculation sheet to the BAS.

NAT 4203-4.2004

Appendix B
Exercise solutions

Day 1: introduction to bookkeeping and accounting

Revision exercise for day 1

1 In the following list indicate which should be classified as an asset, liability, equity, income, cost of sales or expense:

Sales	Income
Wages	Expense
Cash at Bank	Asset
Loan account	Liability
Drawings	Equity
Purchases	Cost of sales
Motor vehicle at cost	Asset
Motor vehicle expenses	Expense
Office equipment	Asset
Repairs and maintenance	Expense

Debtors (accounts receivable)	Asset
Creditors (accounts payable)	Liability
Owner's capital account	Equity
Retained earnings (profits of prior periods)	Equity

2 If I sold you a pair of shoes, do I debit or credit the Sales account? CREDIT

3 If I paid a Western Power bill, do I debit or credit the Electricity account? DEBIT

4 Please fill in the headings in the following general ledger account:

Account name: Motor Vehicle Expenses (Ford Falcon)

Date	Particulars	Debit ($)	Credit ($)	Balance ($)
01/01/YY	Registration	653.28		653.28
01/01/YY	Insurance	1234.78		1888.06

Day 2: analysing transactions and the GST

Exercise 2.1

Date	Account description	Debit ($)	Credit ($)
02/02/YY	Cash at Bank	345.98	
	Cash sales		345.98
03/02/YY	Telephone	267.89	
	Cash at Bank		267.89

Date	Account description	Debit ($)	Credit ($)
15/02/YY	Purchases	234.12	
	Cash at Bank		234.12
26/02/YY	Drawings	897.56	
	Cash at Bank		897.56
30/02/YY	Office furniture	645.00	
	Cash at Bank		645.00

Exercise 2.2

Date	Account description	Debit ($)	Credit ($)
04/02/YY	Debtors	345.98	
	Sales		345.98
16/02/YY	Purchases	234.12	
	Creditors		234.12
27/02/YY	Office furniture	645.00	
	MyOffice		645.00

Exercise 2.3

Account name: Purchases **Folio number: 5100**

Date	Details	Folio	Debit ($)	Credit ($)	Balance ($)
15/02/YY	Cash inventory	GJ1	234.12		234.12

Account name: Drawings **Folio number: 3120**

Date	Details	Folio	Debit ($)	Credit ($)	Balance ($)
26/02/YY	Cash out	GJ1	897.56		897.56

Account name: Office Furniture **Folio number: 1400**

Date	Details	Folio	Debit ($)	Credit ($)	Balance ($)
30/02/YY	Office desk	GJ1	645.00		645.00

Exercise 2.4

Company name: My Company & Sons **GJ1**

Date	Particulars	Folio	Debit ($)	Credit ($)
04/02/YY	Debtors	1200	345.98	
	Sales	4100		345.98
	Being: Sale of goods on credit			
16/02/YY	Purchases	5100	234.12	
	Creditors	2200		234.12
	Being: Purchases on credit			
27/02/YY	Office furniture	1400	645.00	
	MyOffice	2600		645.00
	Being: Purchase of Pam's desk			

Account name: Debtors (Accounts Receivable) **Folio number: 1200**

Date	Details	Folio	Debit ($)	Credit ($)	Balance ($)
4/2/YY	Sales	GJ1	345.98		345.98

Account name: Office Furniture **Folio number: 1400**

Date	Details	Folio	Debit ($)	Credit ($)	Balance ($)
27/2/YY	Front desk	GJ1	645.00		645.00

Account name: Creditors (Accounts Payable) **Folio number: 2200**

Date	Details	Folio	Debit ($)	Credit ($)	Balance ($)
16/2/YY	Widgets Supplies	GJ1		234.12	(234.12)

Account name: MyOffice (Sundry creditor) **Folio number: 2600**

Date	Details	Folio	Debit ($)	Credit ($)	Balance ($)
27/2/YY	Desk #1234	GJ1		645.00	(645.00)

Account name: Sales **Folio number: 4100**

Date	Details	Folio	Debit ($)	Credit ($)	Balance ($)
4/2/YY	Debtors	GJ1		345.98	(345.98)

Account name: Purchases **Folio number: 5100**

Date	Details	Folio	Debit ($)	Credit ($)	Balance ($)
16/2/YY	Widgets	GJ1	234.12		234.12

Trial Balance as at 28/2/YY

Account #	Account name	Debit ($)	Credit ($)
1200	Debtors	345.98	
1400	Office equipment	645.00	
2200	Creditors		234.12
2600	MyOffice		645.00
4100	Sales		345.98
5100	Purchases	234.12	
	TOTALS	1225.10	1225.10

Exercise 2.5

	Yes	No	Why; exempt, input taxed
Domestic rent		X	Exempt
Commercial rent	X		
Wages		X	Not a good or service
Drawings		X	Not a good or service
Electricity	X		
Paid creditor $1200		X	Already accounted for
Council rates		X	Government charges exempt
Received $1500 from J Bloggs on account		X	GST on original transaction
Motor vehicle purchase	X		
Bank charges/Interest		X	Financial charges exempt
Wages on-costs Superannuation		X	Not a good or service
Workers Comp Insurance		X	Not a good or service
PAYG		X	Not a good or service
Capital contribution by owner		X	Can't tax yourself
Motor vehicle contributed by owner		X	Can't tax yourself
Inventory used by owners	X		
Building insurance	X		
Milk for staff coffee		X	Basic foodstuffs exempt
Office furniture	X		
Computer software	X		
Accountant's fees	X		

Revision exercise for day 2

General Journal GJ1

Date	Particulars	Folio	Debit ($)	Credit ($)
01/02/YY	Cash at Bank	1100	10 000.00	
	Capital	3100		10 000.00
	Being: Owner's contribution of capital			
01/02/YY	Cash at Bank	1100	50 000.00	
	Loan account	2200		50 000.00
	Being: Business loan for working capital			
02/02/YY	Motor vehicles	1500	15 000.00	
	GST	2900	1 500.00	
	Cash at Bank	1100		16 500.00
	Being: Purchase of Ford Courier for cash			
02/02/YY	Cash at Bank	1100	345.98	
	Sales	4100		314.53
	GST	2900		31.45
	Being: Cash sales for today			
03/02/YY	Telephone	6800	243.54	
	GST	2900	24.35	
	Cash at Bank	1100		267.89
	Being: Phone bill for January			

Revision exercise for day 2 *(cont'd)*

General Journal *(cont'd)* GJ1

Date	Particulars	Folio	Debit ($)	Credit ($)
04/02/YY	Debtors (Mrs Jones)	1200	325.98	
	Sales	4100		296.35
	GST	2900		29.63
	Being: Credit sale			
15/02/YY	Purchases	5200	212.84	
	GST	2900	21.28	
	Cash at Bank	1100		234.12
	Being: Inventory for the month			
16/02/YY	Purchases	5200	385.57	
	GST	2900	38.55	
	Creditors (Mr Smith)	2100		424.12
	Being: Additional inventory			
26/02/YY	Drawings	3200	897.56	
	Cash at Bank	1100		897.56
	Being: Monthly allowance			
29/02/YY	Creditors (Mr Smith)	2100	424.12	
	Cash at Bank	1100		424.12
	Being: Settlement of our account			

Date	Particulars	Folio	Debit ($)	Credit ($)
30/02/YY	Office furniture	1520	586.37	
	GST	2900	58.63	
	Cash at Bank	1100		645.00
	Being: Purchase of office desk			

Note

- Creditors are also known as Accounts Payable or Trade Payables.
- Debtors are also known as Accounts Receivable or Trade Receivables.
- The GST is accounted for on the initial purchase or sale and not when the account is settled (we'll modify this rule for cash accounting later).
- We are only using the one GST account.
- Where the GST is included in the cost, the amount of GST is obtained by dividing the cost by 11. The amount is not rounded but is truncated. You cannot be asked to pay more GST than the 10 per cent defined by the law.

Account name: Cash at Bank **Folio number: 1100**

Date	Details	Folio	Debit ($)	Credit ($)	Balance ($)
01/02/YY	Capital	GJ1	10 000.00		10 000.00
01/02/YY	Loan	GJ1	50 000.00		60 000.00
02/02/YY	Ford Courier	GJ1		16 500.00	43 500.00

Account name: Cash at Bank *(cont'd)* **Folio number: 1100**

Date	Details	Folio	Debit ($)	Credit ($)	Balance ($)
02/02/YY	Sales	GJ1	345.98		43 845.98
03/02/YY	Telephone	GJ1		267.89	43 578.09
15/02/YY	Cash purchases	GJ1		234.12	43 343.97
26/02/YY	Drawings	GJ1		897.56	42 446.41
29/02/YY	Creditors (Mr Smith)	GJ1		424.12	42 022.29
30/02/YY	Office desk	GJ1		645.00	41 377.29

Account name: Debtor (Mrs Jones) **Folio number: 1200**

Date	Details	Folio	Debit ($)	Credit ($)	Balance ($)
04/02/YY	Sales	GJ1	325.98		325.98

Account name: Motor Vehicle **Folio number: 1500**

Date	Details	Folio	Debit ($)	Credit ($)	Balance ($)
02/02/YY	Cash	GJ1	15 000.00		15 000.00

Account name: Office Furniture **Folio number: 1520**

Date	Details	Folio	Debit ($)	Credit ($)	Balance ($)
30/02/YY	Cash	GJ1	586.37		586.37

Account name: Creditor (Mr Smith) **Folio number: 2100**

Date	Details	Folio	Debit ($)	Credit ($)	Balance ($)
16/02/YY	Purchase	GJ1		424.12	(424.12)
29/02/YY	Cash	GJ1	424.12		

Account name: Loan **Folio number: 2200**

Date	Details	Folio	Debit ($)	Credit ($)	Balance ($)
01/02/YY	Cash	GJ1		50 000.00	(50 000.00)

Account name: GST **Folio number: 2900**

Date	Details	Folio	Debit ($)	Credit ($)	Balance ($)
02/02/YY	Motor vehicle	GJ1	1500.00		1500.00
02/02/YY	Cash sales	GJ1		31.45	1468.55
03/02/YY	Telephone	GJ1	24.35		1492.90
04/02/YY	Sales	GJ1		29.63	1463.27
15/02/YY	Purchases	GJ1	21.28		1484.55
16/02/YY	Purchases	GJ1	38.55		1523.10
30/02/YY	Office furniture	GJ1	58.63		1581.73

Account name: Capital **Folio number: 3100**

Date	Details	Folio	Debit ($)	Credit ($)	Balance ($)
01/02/YY	Cash	GJ1		10 000.00	(10 000.00)

Account name: Drawings **Folio number: 3200**

Date	Details	Folio	Debit ($)	Credit ($)	Balance ($)
26/02/YY	Cash	GJ1	897.56		897.56

Account name: Sales **Folio number: 4100**

Date	Details	Folio	Debit ($)	Credit ($)	Balance ($)
02/02/YY	Cash Sales Summary	GJ1		314.53	(314.53)
04/02/YY	Mrs Jones	GJ1		296.35	(610.88)

Account name: Purchases **Folio number: 5200**

Date	Details	Folio	Debit ($)	Credit ($)	Balance ($)
15/02/YY	Cash	GJ1	212.84		212.84
16/02/YY	Mr Smith	GJ1	385.57		598.41

Account name: Telephone **Folio number: 6800**

Date	Details	Folio	Debit ($)	Credit ($)	Balance ($)
03/02/YY	Cash	GJ1	243.54		243.54

Trial Balance as at 28/02/YY

Account #	Account name	Debit ($)	Credit ($)
1100	Cash at Bank	41 377.29	
1200	Debtors	325.98	
1500	Motor Vehicle	15 000.00	
1520	Office Furniture	586.37	
2200	Loan		50 000.00
2900	GST	1 581.73	
3100	Capital		10 000.00
3200	Drawings	897.56	
4100	Sales		610.88
5200	Purchases	598.41	
6800	Telephone	243.54	
	TOTALS	60 610.88	60 610.88

If we were to carry on and create the income statement and balance sheet, then the result would be:

Income statement for the period 1/2/YY to 28/2/YY

Income

Sales	610.88
Total income	**$610.88**

***Less* cost of goods sold**	
Purchases	598.41
Gross profit from trading	**$ 12.47 (2.01% margin)**
***Less* expenses**	
Telephone	243.54
Net loss from trading	**($231.07)**

Balance sheet as at 28/02/YY (also called statement of financial position: A = L + E)

Assets	**$**	**$**	**$**
Current assets			
Cash at Bank	41 377.29		
Debtors	325.98	41 703.27	
Noncurrent (fixed) assets			
Motor vehicle	15 000.00		
Office furniture	586.37	15 586.37	
Total assets		**$57 289.64**	
Liabilities			
Current liabilities			
GST	(1 581.73)		
Noncurrent (long-term) liabilities			
Loan	50 000.00		
Total liabilities		**48 418.27**	
Proprietorship *(equity)*			
Capital contribution	10 000.00		
Drawings	(897.56)		
Retained earnings (from income statement)	(231.07)	**8 871.37**	
Total liabilities and proprietorship			**$57 289.64**

Note

- These reports were not part of the original question but are included here for completeness.
- I have put the common name italised in brackets; for example, *(equity)*.
- Reports are normally in whole dollars, or even thousands of dollars.
- The GST is in debit but as it would normally be in credit I have left it as a current liability. In practice the GST is accounted for prior to year's end and would not normally appear in your reports.
- Drawings and loss are both debit entries but are in brackets. This is because proprietorship is by nature a credit amount and therefore the () indicate the opposite—that is, a debit entry.

Day 3: cash transactions

Exercise 3.1

Note

The total of the debits always equals the total of the credits. The column names used are not fixed. You can use as many as necessary and for any recurring transactions.

Cash Payments Journal

CP1

Date	Chq #	Particulars	Amount (Bank; $)	Accounts payable ($)	Cash purchases ($)	GST (paid; $)	Other payments		Folio (creditors)
							Amount ($)	Details	
08/01/YY	456	Telstra	330.00			30.00	300.00	Phone	Dr
10/01/YY	457	West Electricity	110.00			10.00	100.00	Electricity	Dr
15/01/YY	458	Stores Pty Ltd	1650.00		1500.00	150.00			Dr
28/01/YY	459	MyAds	660.00			60.00	600.00	Advertising	
29/01/YY	460	Cash	200.00				200.00	Wages	
		TOTALS	2950.00		1500.00	250.00	1200.00		
		FOLIO	Cr	Dr	Dr	Dr			

(Cash inventory purchases)

Cash Receipts Journal

CR1

Date	Rec #	Particulars	Amount (Bank; $)	Accounts receivable ($)	Fees ($)	GST (collected; $)	Other receipts		Folio (debtors)
							Amount ($)	Details	
08/01/YY	230	L Smith	880.00		800.00	80.00			
10/01/YY	Bank	WestBank	430.00				430.00	Interest	Cr
15/01/YY	231	R Rogers	1000.00	1000.00					Cr
29/01/YY	232	R Brown	770.00		700.00	70.00			Cr
		TOTALS	3080.00	1000.00	1500.00	150.00	430.00		
		FOLIO	Dr	Cr	Cr	Cr			

(Cash inventory sales)

Revision exercise for day 3

Cash Payments Journal

CP1

Date	Chq #	Particulars	Amount (Bank; $)	Accounts payable ($)	Cash purchases ($)	GST (paid; $)	Other payments		Folio (creditors)
							Amount ($)	Details	
02/05/YY	123	Cash purchase	10000.00		9000.00	1000.00			Dr
03/05/YY	124	West Electricity	440.00			40.00	400.00	Electricity	Dr 6140
04/05/YY	125	My Landlord	1100.00			100.00	1000.00	Rent	Dr 6160
06/05/YY	Bank	WestBank	150.00				150.00	Bank fees	Dr 6120
07/05/YY	126	J Bloggs	1500.00				1500.00	Drawings	Dr 3300
09/05/YY	127	Widgets & Co	1500.00	1500.00					Dr
21/05/YY	128	MyOffice Pty Ltd	495.00				495.00	Computer	Dr 2700
22/05/YY	129	My Landlord	275.00			25.00	250.00	Rent	Dr 6160
		TOTALS	15460.00	1500.00	9000.00	1165.00	3795.00		
		FOLIO	Cr 1100	Dr 2500	Dr 5100	Dr 2100			

(Cash inventory purchases)

Cash Receipts Journal

CR1

Date	Rec #	Particulars	Amount (Bank; $)	Accounts receivable ($)	Fees ($)	GST (collected; $)	Other receipts		Folio (debtors)
							Amount ($)	Details	
01/05/YY	Bank	Owners	30 000.00				30 000.00	Capital	Cr 3100
05/05/YY	Bank	ATO	500.00				500.00	TAX Refund	Cr 7100
08/05/YY	Till	Cash sales	550.00		500.00	50.00			Cr
20/05/YY	567	Mr Smith	1 600.00	1 600.00					Cr
23/05/YY	Till	Cash sales	990.00		900.00	90.00			Cr
24/05/YY	Bank	WestBank	10 000.00				10 000.00	WestBank Loan	Cr 2200
		TOTALS	43 640.00	1 600.00	1 400.00	140.00	40 500.00		
		FOLIO	Dr 1100	Cr 1500	Cr 4100	Cr 2100			

(Cash inventory sales)

General Journal **CP1**

Date	Particulars	Folio	Debit ($)	Credit ($)
21/5/YY	Office equipment	1800	3000.00	
	GST	2100	300.00	
	MyOffice Pty Ltd	2700		3300.00
	Being: Purchase of office computer			

Account name: Cash at Bank **Folio number: 1100**

Date	Details	Folio	Debit ($)	Credit ($)	Balance ($)
31/5/YY	Cash receipts	CR1	43 640.00		43 640.00
31/5/YY	Cash payments	CP1		15 460.00	28 180.00

Account name: Accounts Receivable (debtors) **Folio number: 1500**

Date	Details	Folio	Debit ($)	Credit ($)	Balance ($)
31/5/YY	Cash receipts	CR1		1600.00	(1600.00)

Account name: Office Equipment **Folio number: 1800**

Date	Details	Folio	Debit ($)	Credit ($)	Balance ($)
21/5/YY	MyOffice	GJ1	3000.00		3000.00

Account name: GST **Folio number: 2100**

Date	Details	Folio	Debit ($)	Credit ($)	Balance ($)
21/5/YY	Asset purchase	GJ1	300.00		300.00
31/5/YY	Cash payments	CP1	1165.00		1465.00
31/5/YY	Cash receipts	CR1		140.00	1325.00

(Note: refund due)

Account name: WestBank Loan **Folio number: 2200**

Date	Details	Folio	Debit ($)	Credit ($)	Balance ($)
24/5/YY	Cash receipts	CR1		10 000.00	10 000.00

Account name: Accounts Payable (creditors) Folio number: 2500

Date	Details	Folio	Debit ($)	Credit ($)	Balance ($)
31/5/YY	Cash payments	CP1	1500.00		1500.00

Account name: MyOffice (Sundry Creditor) Folio number: 2700

Date	Details	Folio	Debit ($)	Credit ($)	Balance ($)
21/5/YY	Computer	GJ1		3300.00	(3300.00)
21/5/YY	Deposit paid	CP1	495.00		(2805.00)

Account name: Capital J Bloggs Folio number: 3100

Date	Details	Folio	Debit ($)	Credit ($)	Balance ($)
01/5/YY	Owners equity	CR1		30 000.00	30 000.00

Account name: Drawings J Bloggs Folio number: 3300

Date	Details	Folio	Debit ($)	Credit ($)	Balance ($)
07/5/YY	J Bloggs	CP1	1500.00		1500.00

Account name: Sales Folio number: 4100

Date	Details	Folio	Debit ($)	Credit ($)	Balance ($)
31/5/YY	Cash receipts	CR1		1400.00	(1400.00)

Account name: Purchases Folio number: 5100

Date	Details	Folio	Debit ($)	Credit ($)	Balance ($)
31/5/YY	Cash purchases	CP1	9000.00		9000.00

Account name: Bank Fees Folio number: 6120

Date	Details	Folio	Debit ($)	Credit ($)	Balance ($)
06/5/YY	WestBank	CP1	150.00		150.00

Account name: Electricity **Folio number: 6140**

Date	Details	Folio	Debit ($)	Credit ($)	Balance ($)
03/5/YY	West Electricity	CP1	400.00		400.00

Account name: Rent **Folio number: 6160**

Date	Details	Folio	Debit ($)	Credit ($)	Balance ($)
04/5/YY	My Landlord	CP1	1000.00		1000.00
22/5/YY	My Landlord	CP1	250.00		1250.00

Account name: Miscellaneous Income **Folio number: 7100**

Date	Details	Folio	Debit ($)	Credit ($)	Balance ($)
05/5/YY	Tax refund ATO	CR1		500.00	30 000.00

Trial Balance as at 31/05/YY

Account #	Account name	Debit ($)	Credit ($)
1100	Cash at Bank	28 180.00	
1500	Accounts receivable (Debtors)*		1 600.00
1800	Office equipment	3 000.00	
2100	GST	1 325.00	
2200	WestBank loan		10 000.00
2500	Accounts payable (Creditors)*	1 500.00	
2700	MyOffice Pty Ltd		2 805.00
3100	Capital J Bloggs		30 000.00
3300	Drawings J Bloggs	1 500.00	
4100	Sales		1 400.00
5100	Purchases	9 000.00	

Account #	Account name	Debit ($)	Credit ($)
6120	Bank fees	150.00	
6140	Electricity	400.00	
6160	Rent	1 250.00	
7100	Miscellaneous income		500.00
	TOTALS	46 305.00	46 305.00

(Debits must equal the credits)

*These are amounts paid off the accounts

Note

All of the entries appear in chart of account number order.

Day 4: proving our accounting records

Exercise 4.1

WestBank Ltd

14 Anywhere Street, LinconVille WA 6999

MyBusiness Pty Ltd — **June YY**
PO Box 123 — **No 57**
LinconVille WA 6999

Date	Particulars	Debit ($)	Credit ($)	Balance ($)		
01/06/YY	Opening Balance			95 599.78	Cr	✓
01/06/YY	Deposit		990.00	96 589.78	Cr	✓
04/06/YY	Cheque 130	11 000.00		85 589.78	Cr	✓
06/06/YY	Cheque 132	990.00		84 599.78	Cr	✓
07/06/YY	Cheque 133	1500.00		83 099.78	Cr	✓
09/06/YY	Deposit		550.00	83 649.78	Cr	✓
13/06/YY	Interest on Deposit		(1 200.00)	84 849.78	Cr	
15/06/YY	Cheque 131	440.00		84 409.78	Cr	✓
15/06/YY	BHP Dividend		(1 256.00)	85 665.78	Cr	
24/06/YY	Deposit		1 980.00	87 645.78	Cr	✓
24/06/YY	Cheque 136	3 300.00		84 345.78	Cr	✓
27/06/YY	Cheque 135	990.00		83 355.78	Cr	✓
29/06/YY	Bank Fee	(66.00)		83 289.78	Cr	

Cash Payments Journal

CP1

Date	Chq #	Particulars	Amount (Bank; $)		Accounts payable ($)	Cash purchases ($)	GST (paid; $)	Other payments		Folio (creditors)
								Amount ($)	Details	
02/06/YY	130	J Smith	11 000.00	✓		10 000.00	1 000.00			Dr
03/06/YY	131	West Electricity	440.00	✓			40.00	400.00	Electricity	Dr 6300
04/06/YY	132	My Landlord	990.00	✓			90.00	900.00	Rent	Dr 4700
07/06/YY	133	J Bloggs	1 500.00	✓				1 500.00	Drawings	Dr 3300
09/06/YY	134	Widgets & Co	2 200.00		2 200.00					Dr
22/06/YY	135	My Landlord	990.00	✓			90.00	900.00	Rent	Dr 4700
24/06/YY	136	Cash	3 300.00	✓				3 300.00	Wages	Dr 6900
29/06/YY	BANK	Bank Fee	66.00	✓				66.00	Fees & Charges	Dr 6800
		TOTALS	20 486.00		2 200.00	10 000.00	1 220.00	7 066.00		
		FOLIO	Cr 1100		Dr 2100	Dr	Dr 2900			

(Cash inventory purchases)

Cash Receipts Journal

CR1

Date	Rec #	Particulars	Amount (Bank; $)		Accounts receivable ($)	Fees ($)	GST (collected; $)	Other receipts		Folio (debtors)
								Amount ($)	Details	
08/06/YY		Till—Cash Sales Summary	550.00	✓		500.00	50.00			
23/06/YY		Till—Cash Sales Summary	1980.00	✓		1800.00	180.00			Cr
28/06/YY		Till—Cash Sales Summary	880.00			800.00	80.00			Cr
13/06/YY	Bank	Interest	1200.00	✓				1200.00	Interest	Cr 8400
15/06/YY	Bank	BHP	1256.00	✓				1256.00	Dividend	Cr 8300
		TOTALS	5866.00			3100.00	310.00	2456.00		
		FOLIO	Dr 1100		Cr	Cr 4100	Cr 2900			

(Cash inventory sales)

Account name: Cash at Bank **Folio number: 1100**

Date	Details	Folio	Debit ($)	Credit ($)	Balance ($)
01/05/YY	Opening Balance		67 889.78		67 889.78
31/05/YY	Cash Deposits	CR1	43 640.00		111 529.78
31/05/YY	Cash Receipts	CP1		15 435.00	96 094.78
30/06/YY	Cash Deposits	CR2	5 866.00		101 960.78
30/06/YY	Cash Payments	CP2		20 486.00	81 474.78

Bank Reconciliation as at 30/06/YY

Closing balance of the bank statement **$83 289.78 CR**

***Plus* outstanding deposit of 26/06/YY** **$880.00**

***Less* unpresented cheques:**

Cheque number	Amount
128	495.00
134	2200.00

$2 695.00

Closing balance of general ledger Cash at Bank account **$81 474.78 DR**

Revision exercise for day 4

Cash Payments Journal CP1

Date	Chq #	Particulars	Amount (Bank; $)	
02/07/YY	137	Inventory	9000.00	✓
03/07/YY	138	Electricity	330.00	✓
04/07/YY	139	Mr Bloggs	1500.00	✓
05/07/YY	140	Rent	990.00	✓
22/07/YY	141	Rent	990.00	
24/07/YY	142	Wages	3300.00	✓
29/07/YY	Bank	Fee	66.00	✓
		TOTALS	16176.00	
		FOLIO	Cr	

Cash Receipts Journal CR1

Date	Rec #	Particulars	Amount (Bank; $)	
08/07/YY	Cash Sales Summary	Cash	660.00	✓
23/07/YY	Cash Sales Summary	Cash	330.00	✓
28/07/YY	Cash Sales Summary	Cash	1650.00	
		TOTALS	2640.00	
		FOLIO	Dr	

Account name: Cash at Bank **Folio number: 1100**

Date	Details	Folio	Debit ($)	Credit ($)	Balance ($)
01/07/YY	Opening Balance				81474.78
31/07/YY	Cash Payments	CP1		16176.00	64704.78
31/07/YY	Cash Receipts	CR1	2640.00		67938.78

Bank Reconciliation as at 31/07/YY

<u>Closing</u> balance of the bank statement		**$67 278.78 CR**
***Plus* outstanding deposit of 28/07/YY**		**$1 650.00**
***Less* unpresented cheques:**		
Cheque number	**Amount**	
141	990.00	
<u>Closing</u> balance of general ledger Cash at Bank account		**$67 938.78 CR**

Day 5: crediting accounts

Exercise 5.1

2 Oct YY Mr Jones pays a deposit of $1320 for the ticket on the *Western Sun*. He also requests three tours with City Tours to be included.

Ticket cost: $2160 *GST: $480* *Deposit: $1320*

Analysis: This transaction is actually made in two parts. Firstly we have a credit sale of the tickets and then a cash deposit received. Credit sales are recorded through the sales journal and deposits received through the cash receipts journal.

Both amounts are then posted individually to Mr Jones's account. The totals of the journal columns will only be posted to the general ledger at the month's end.

3 Oct YY Western Sun Ticketing confirms the availability and issues an invoice. We pay a 25 per cent deposit.

Our cost: $1800 *GST: $180* *Deposit: $495*

Analysis: This transaction is again made in two parts. Firstly we have a credit purchase of the tickets and then a cash deposit paid. Credit purchases are recorded through the purchases journal and deposits paid through the cash payments journal.

Both amounts are then posted to the Western Sun Ticketing account.

4 Oct YY City Tours accepts our booking for Mr Jones subject to sufficient numbers.

What is required of us? Nothing

Analysis: This is not as yet a business transaction but rather just a request. At this stage there is no legal obligation to pay or receive money. It is only when the contract is made that we are required to enter the details into our records.

7 Oct YY City Tours confirms the Albany and Bunbury tours but the Esperance tour is cancelled due to insufficient numbers. We receive its invoice. Mr Jones is informed and asked to make his final payment.

Our cost: $1200 *GST: $120* *Deposit: $1760*

Analysis: This is again a two-sided transaction. In this case we have received an invoice from City Tours. It is now our creditor and as such the invoice is recorded in our purchases journal as a credit purchase. The other side of the transaction is a credit sale. Mr Jones offered to purchase City Tours from us and now we can accept his offer. The credit sale to Mr Jones is recorded in the sales journal.

The amounts are then posted to the appropriate debtor's (Mr Jones) and creditor's (City Tours) accounts.

10 Oct YY Final settlement is received from Mr Jones.

Cost of cruise: $1320 Cost of tours: $1760

Analysis: This payment by Mr Jones is recorded in the cash receipts journal in settlement of Mr Jones's account.

The payment is also posted to Mr Jones's account settling the debt.

14 Oct YY Final payment is made to Western Sun Ticketing and City Tours.

Cost of cruise: $1485 Cost of tours: $1320

Analysis: These payments are recorded in the cash payments journal, one for Western Sun Ticketing and one for City Tours, in full settlement of their accounts.

The amounts are then posted to the appropriate creditor's accounts, one for Western Sun Ticketing and one for City Tours.

Sales Journal **SJ1**

Date	Invoice	Particulars (debtor's acct to be debited)	Debtors ledger folio	Accounts receivable ($)	Credit sales ($)	GST (collected; $)
02/10/YY		Mr Jones 30/10	DL1	2640.00	2400.00	240.00
07/10/YY		Mr Jones's tours	DL1	1760.00	1600.00	160.00

Cash Receipts Journal **CR1**

Date	Rec #	Particulars	Amount (Bank; $)	Accounts receivable ($)	Folio
02/10/YY		Mr Jones	1320.00	1320.00	D1
10/10/YY		Mr Jones	3080.00	3080.00	D1

Purchases Journal

PJ1

Date	Invoice	Particulars (creditor's acct to be debited)	Creditors ledger folio	Accounts payable ($)	Credit purchases ($)	GST (paid; $)
03/10/YY	345	Western Sun Ticketing	CL1	1980.00	1800.00	180.00
07/10/YY		City Tours	CL2	1320.00	1200.00	120.00

Cash Payments Journal

CP1

Date	Chq #	Particulars	Amount (Bank; $)	Accounts Payable ($)	Folio
03/10/YY	123	Western Sun Ticketing	495.00	495.00	CL1
14/10/YY	124	Western Sun Ticketing	1485.00	1485.00	CL1
14/10/YY	125	City Tours	1320.00	1320.00	CL1

Debtors Ledger

Debtor's name **Mr Jones** **DL1**

Date	Details	Folio	Debit ($)	Credit ($)	Balance ($)
02/10/YY	Western Sun Ticketing 30/10	SJ1	2640.00		2640.00
02/10/YY	Deposit paid	CR1		1320.00	1320.00
07/10/YY	City Tours	SJ1	1760.00		3080.00
10/10/YY	Final payment	CR1		3080.00	0.00

Creditors Ledger

Creditor's name Western Sun Ticketing **CL1**

Date	Details	Folio	Debit ($)	Credit ($)	Balance ($)
03/10/YY	Western Sun Ticketing 30/10	PJ1		1980.00	(1880.00)
03/10/YY	Deposit paid	CP1	495.00		(1485.00)
14/10/YY	Final settlement	CP1	1485.00		0.00

Creditors Ledger

Creditor's name City Tours **CL1**

Date	Details	Folio	Debit ($)	Credit ($)	Balance ($)
07/10/YY	City Tours 30/10	PJ1		1320.00	(1320.00)
14/10/YY	Final settlement	CP1	1320.00		0.00

Exercise 5.2

Exercise 5.1 revisted as a cash accounting exercise.

2 Oct YY Mr Jones pays a deposit of $1320 for the ticket on the *Western Sun*. He also requests three tours with City Tours to be included.

Ticket cost: $2160 *GST: $480* *Deposit: $1320*

Analysis: This transaction is actually made in two parts. Firstly we have a credit sale of the tickets and then a cash deposit received. The credit sale is recorded in Mr Jones's account. There is no record made in our accounts of this 'non-cash' transaction.

Since the deposit paid is a cash receipt, it is recorded in our cash receipts journal. However, no sales or GST amount has previously been recorded for this amount and no Accounts Receivable amount raised. Therefore, the amount is entered into the Sales and GST columns (not the debtors column as in accrual accounting—there are no debtors or creditors in cash accounting).

3 Oct YY Western Sun Ticketing confirms the availability and issues an invoice. We pay a 25 per cent deposit.

Our cost: $1800 *GST: $180* *Deposit: $495*

Analysis: This transaction is again made in two parts. Firstly we have a credit purchase of the tickets and then a cash deposit paid.

The creditor's ledger account for Western Sun Ticketing is updated with the credit purchase amount but the credit purchase is not recorded in our general accounts. There is no purchases journal in cash accounting.

The deposit paid is recorded in the cash payments journal in the Purchases and GST columns. Again the creditor's ledger account for Western Sun Ticketing is updated with the amount paid.

4 Oct YY City Tours accepts our booking for Mr Jones subject to sufficient numbers.

What is required of us? Nothing.

Analysis: This is not as yet a business transaction but rather just a request. At this stage there is no legal obligation to pay or receive money. It is only when the contract is made that we are required to enter the details into our records.

7 Oct YY City Tours confirms the Albany and Bunbury tours but the Esperance tour is cancelled due to insufficient numbers. We receive its invoice. Mr Jones is informed and asked to make his final payment.

Our cost: $1200 *GST: $120* *Deposit: $1760*

Analysis: This is again a two-sided transaction. In this case we have received an invoice from City Tours. It is now our creditor and as such the invoice is recorded in the creditor's ledger but not in the general accounts.

The other side of the transaction is a credit sale. Mr Jones offered to purchase City Tours from us and now we can accept his offer. The credit sale to Mr Jones is recorded in his debtor's ledger account.

There are no amounts of cash changing hands in this transaction and therefore no amounts are recorded in the general accounts.

10 Oct YY Final settlement is received from Mr Jones.

Cost of cruise: $1320 Cost of tours: $1760

Analysis: This payment by Mr Jones is recorded in the cash receipts journal in settlement of Mr Jones's account; however, in cash accounting it is recorded in the Sales and GST columns, not against the Accounts Receivable.

The payment is also posted to Mr Jones's account to settle the debt.

14 Oct YY Final payment is made to Western Sun Ticketing and City Tours.

Cost of cruise: $1485 Cost of tours: $1320

Analysis: These payments are recorded in the cash payments journal, one for Western Sun Ticketing and one for City Tours, in full settlement of their accounts. However, they are posted as Purchases with GST, not against Accounts Payable.

The amounts are then posted to the appropriate creditor's accounts, one for Western Sun Ticketing and one for City Tours.

Debtors Ledger

Debtor's name Mr Jones **DL1**

Date	Details	Folio	Debit ($)	Credit ($)	Balance ($)
02/10/YY	Western Sun Ticketing 30/10		2640.00		2640.00
02/10/YY	Deposit paid	CR1		1320.00	1320.00
07/10/YY	City Tours		1760.00		3080.00
10/10/YY	Final payment	CR1		3080.00	0.00

Creditors Ledger

Creditor's name Western Sun Ticketing **CL1**

Date	Details	Folio	Debit ($)	Credit ($)	Balance ($)
03/10/YY	Western Sun Ticketing 30/10			1980.00	(1880.00)
03/10/YY	Deposit paid	CP1	495.00		(1485.00)
14/10/YY	Final settlement	CP1	1485.00		0.00

Creditors Ledger

Creditor's name City Tours **CL1**

Date	Details	Folio	Debit ($)	Credit ($)	Balance ($)
07/10/YY	City Tours 30/10			1320.00	(1320.00)
14/10/YY	Final settlement	CP1	1320.00		0.00

Cash Receipts Journal **CR1**

Date	Rec #	Particulars	Amount (Bank; $)	Sales ($)	GST (collected; $)	Folio
02/10/YY		Mr Jones	1320.00	2400.00	240.00	D1
10/10/YY		Mr Jones	3080.00	1600.00	160.00	D1
		TOTALS	4400.00	4000.00	400.00	

Cash Payments Journal **CP1**

Date	Chq #	Particulars	Amount (Bank; $)	Purchases ($)	GST (paid; $)	Folio
03/10/YY	123	Western Sun Ticketing	495.00	450.00	45.00	CL1
14/10/YY	124	Western Sun Ticketing	1485.00	1350.00	135.00	CL1
14/10/YY	125	City Tours	1320.00	1200.00	120.00	CL1
		TOTALS	3300.00	3000.00	300.00	

Account name: GST **Folio number: 2900**

Date	Details	Folio	Debit ($)	Credit ($)	Balance ($)
31/10/YY	Monthly cash purchases	CP1	300.00		300.00
31/10/YY	Monthly cash sales	CR1		400.00	(100.00)

Account name: Sales **Folio number: 4100**

Date	Details	Folio	Debit ($)	Credit ($)	Balance ($)
31/10/YY	Monthly cash sales	CR1		4000.00	(4000.00)

Account name: Purchases **Folio number: 5100**

Date	Details	Folio	Debit ($)	Credit ($)	Balance ($)
31/10/YY	Monthly cash purchases	CP1	3000.00		3000.00

Revision exercise for day 5

Creditors Ledger

Creditor's name Mrs Whacko **CL1**

Date	Details	Folio	Debit ($)	Credit ($)	Balance ($)
15/09/YY	Invoice 1356			1650.00	(1650.00)
15/10/YY	Invoice 1478			1320.00	(2970.00)
30/10/YY	Cheque 156 for invoice 1356	CP1	1650.00		(1320.00)
15/11/YY	Invoice 1498			1320.00	(2640.00)
30/11/YY	Cheque 157 for invoice 1478	CP1	1320.00		(1320.00)
15/12/YY	Invoice 1527			1320.00	(2640.00)
22/12/YY	Adjustment note 67823 for invoice 1527		330.00		(2310.00)
23/12/YY	Cheque 158 for invoice 1498	CP1	1320.00		(990.00)
15/01/YY	Invoice 1564			1870.00	(2860.00)
28/01/YY	Cheque 159 for invoice 1257	CP1	990.00		(1870.00)
15/02/YY	Invoice 1608			990.00	(2860.00)
01/03/YY	Cheque 160 for invoice 1564	CP1	1870.00		(990.00)
15/03/YY	Invoice 1628			1980.00	(2970.00)
28/03/YY	Cheque 161 for invoice 1698	CP1	990.00		(1980.00)
28/03/YY	Adjustment note 68945 for invoice 1628		660.00		(1320.00)
15/04/YY	Invoice 1676			1320.00	(2640.00)
01/05/YY	Cheque 162 for invoice 1628	CP1	1320.00		(1320.00)

Date	Details	Folio	Debit ($)	Credit ($)	Balance ($)
15/05/YY	Invoice 1801			1980.00	(3300.00)
30/05/YY	Cheque 163 for invoice 1676	CP1	1320.00		(1980.00)
15/06/YY	Invoice 1821			1320.00	(3300.00)
30/06/YY	Cheque 164 for invoice 1801	CP1	1980.00		(1320.00)

Note

The balance reflects that we are only outstanding for invoice 1821, which is still within the 45-day period. If you have a trusted supplier, it is good business practice to periodically reconcile your creditors ledger with their debtors ledger to ensure that everything is 100 per cent consistent. It is easier to fix a problem as it happens than try to fix it months later.

Cash Payments Journal **CP1**

Date	Chq #	Particulars	Amount (Bank; $)	Purchases ($)	GST (paid; $)	Folio
30/10/YY	156	Whacko	1650.00	1500.00	150.00	CL1
30/11/YY	157	Whacko	1320.00	1200.00	120.00	CL1
23/12/YY	158	Whacko	1320.00	1200.00	120.00	CL1
28/01/YY	159	Whacko	990.00	900.00	90.00	CL1
01/03/YY	160	Whacko	1870.00	1700.00	170.00	CL1
28/03/YY	161	Whacko	990.00	900.00	90.00	CL1

Cash Payments Journal *(cont'd)* CP1

Date	Chq #	Particulars	Amount (Bank; $)	Purchases ($)	GST (paid; $)	Folio
01/05/YY	162	Whacko	1320.00	1200.00	120.00	CL1
30/05/YY	163	Whacko	1320.00	1200.00	120.00	CL1
30/06/YY	164	Whacko	1980.00	1800.00	180.00	CL1

Account name: GST **Folio number: 2900**

Date	Details	Folio	Debit ($)	Credit ($)	Balance ($)
30/10/YY	Invoice 1356	CP1	150.00		150.00
30/11/YY	Invoice 1478	CP1	120.00		270.00
23/12/YY	Invoice 1498	CP1	120.00		390.00
28/01/YY	Invoice 1257	CP1	90.00		480.00
01/03/YY	Invoice 1564	CP1	170.00		650.00
28/03/YY	Invoice 1608	CP1	90.00		740.00
01/05/YY	Invoice 1628	CP1	120.00		860.00
30/05/YY	Invoice 1676	CP1	120.00		980.00
30/06/YY	Invoice 1801	CP1	180.00		1160.00

Account name: Purchases **Folio number: 5100**

Date	Details	Folio	Debit ($)	Credit ($)	Balance ($)
30/10/YY	Invoice 1356	CP1	1500.00		1500.00
30/11/YY	Invoice 1478	CP1	1200.00		2700.00
23/12/YY	Invoice 1498	CP1	1200.00		3900.00
28/01/YY	Invoice 1257	CP1	900.00		4800.00
01/03/YY	Invoice 1564	CP1	1700.00		6500.00

Date	Details	Folio	Debit ($)	Credit ($)	Balance ($)
28/03/YY	Invoice 1608	CP1	900.00		7 400.00
01/05/YY	Invoice 1628	CP1	1 200.00		8 600.00
30/05/YY	Invoice 1676	CP1	1 200.00		9 800.00
30/06/YY	Invoice 1801	CP1	1 800.00		11 600.00

Day 6: completing your quarterly BAS

Exercise 6.1

		December Qtr ($)		March Qtr ($)		Difference ($)		GST ($)	
		Dr	Cr	Dr	Cr	Dr	Cr	Dr	Cr
1100	Bank	38 307		45 693		~~7386~~			
1300	Motor Vehicles	15 423		15 423		0			
1400	Office Equipment	12 566		12 566		0			
1450	Office Computers			3 478		3 478		348	
2100	Bank Loan		25 456	0	19 833	~~5623~~			
2900	GST		1826	0	1 186	~~640~~			
3110	Capital		25 000		35 000		~~10 000~~		
3120	Drawings	14 560		21 138		~~6578~~			
3200	Retained Earnings	0			0		0		
4100	Sales		190 123		285 796		95 673		9 566

Exercise 6.1 *(cont'd)*

		December Qtr ($)		March Qtr ($)		Difference ($)		GST ($)	
		Dr	Cr	Dr	Cr	Dr	Cr	Dr	Cr
5100	Purchases	153 449		231 872		78 423		7 842	
6100	Advertising	1 350		1 850		500		50	
6150	Power	400		600		200		20	
6170	Interest paid	3 950		5 595		~~1645~~			
6190	Office Rent	2 400		3 600		1 200		120	
	TOTALS	242 405	242 405	341 815	341 815	105673	105673	8 380	9 566
							GST Payable		1186

G1	Total sales	**$95 673**
G10	Capital purchases	**$3478**
G11	Non-capital purchases	**$80 323 (78 423 + 500 + 200 + 1200)**
1A	GST on sales	**$9566 (10% of 95 673)**
1B	GST on purchases	**$8380 (10% of 80 323 + 3478)**

Difference = GST payable. Does it reconcile with your GST account? **$1186**

Revision exercise for day 6

For the June quarter I made the following business transactions:

- I paid $1186 to the Tax Office for GST outstanding.

  Dr GST $1186

  Cr Cash at Bank $1186

- I purchased a new office computer for $3300 (including GST) of which a third is considered to be for private use.

  Dr Office Computers $2000

  Dr GST $200

  Dr Capital $1100 (alternative new 3150 Private Use account)

  Cr Cash at Bank $3300

- I paid $5600 off my bank loan.

  Dr Bank Loan $5600

  Cr Cash at Bank $5600

- I withdrew $5500 for private use.

  Dr Drawings $5500

  Cr Cash at Bank $5500

- I made $82 940 in sales.

  Dr Cash at Bank $82 940

  Cr Sales $75 400

  Cr GST $7540

- I purchased $62 150 of goods.

  Dr Purchases $56 500

  Dr GST $5650

  Cr Cash at Bank $62 150

- I spent $429 on advertising.

  Dr Advertising $390

  Dr GST $39

  Cr Cash at Bank $429

- I paid $220 for electricity.

  Dr Advertising $390

  Dr GST $39

  Cr Cash at Bank $429

- I paid $1037 in interest charges.

  Dr Interest $1037

  Cr Cash at Bank $1037

- I paid $1320 on office rent.

  Dr Rent $1200

  Dr GST $120

  Cr Cash at Bank $1320

> **Note**
>
> At this point you should enter all of the above transactions into the appropriate journals, post them to the ledgers and then produce a trial balance. I'm going to shortcut this and just add a posting column to our worksheet.

		March Qtr ($)		June Expenses ($)		June Trial Balance ($)	
		Dr	Cr	Dr	Cr	Dr	Cr
1100	Bank	45 693		82 940	80 742	47 891	0
1300	Motor Vehicles	15 423				15 423	0
1400	Office Equipment	12 566				12 566	0
1450	Office Computers	3 478		2 000		5 478	0
2100	Bank Loan		19 833	5 600		0	14 233
2900	GST		1 186	7 215	7 540	0	1 511
3110	Capital		35 000	1 100		0	33 900
3120	Drawings	21 138		5 500		26 638	0

		March Qtr ($)		June Expenses ($)		June Trial Balance ($)	
		Dr	Cr	Dr	Cr	Dr	Cr
3200	Retained Earnings					0	0
4100	Sales		285 796		75 400	0	361 196
5100	Purchases	231 872		56 500		288 372	0
6100	Advertising	1 850		390		2 240	0
6150	Power	600		200		800	0
6170	Interest paid	5 595		1 037		6 632	0
6190	Office Rent	3 600		1 200		4 800	0
	TOTALS	341 815	341 815	163 682	163 682	410 840	410 840

		March Qtr ($)		June Trial Balance ($)		Difference ($)		GST	
		Dr	Cr	Dr	Cr	Dr	Cr		
1100	Bank	45 693		47 891	0	~~2 198~~	0		
1300	Motor Vehicles	15 423		15 423	0	0	0	0	0
1400	Office Equipment	12 566		12 566	0	0	0	0	0
1450	Office Computers	3 478		5 478	0	2 000	0	200	0
2100	Bank Loan		19 833	0	14 233	~~5 600~~	0		
2900	GST		1 186	0	1 511	0	~~325~~		
3110	Capital		35 000	0	33 900	~~1 100~~	0		
3120	Drawings	21 138		26 638	0	~~5 500~~	0		
3200	Retained Earnings			0	0	0	0		

		March Qtr ($)		June Trial Balance ($)		Difference ($)		GST	
		Dr	Cr	Dr	Cr	Dr	Cr		
4100	Sales		285 796	0	361 196	0	75 400	0	7 540
5100	Purchases	231 872		288 372	0	56 500	0	5650	0
6100	Advertising	1 850		2 240	0	390	0	39	0
6150	Power	600		800	0	200	0	20	0
6170	Interest paid	5 595		6 632	0	~~1 037~~	0		
6190	Office Rent	3 600		4 800	0	1 200	0	120	0
	TOTALS	341 815	341 815	410 840	410 840	75 725	75 725	6029	7540
							GST Payable		1511

Required:

G1	Total sales	**$75 400**
G10	Capital purchases	**$2000**
G11	Non-capital purchases	**$58 290 (56 500 + 390 + 200 + 1200)**
1A	GST on sales	**$7540 (10% of 75 400)**
1B	GST on purchases	**$6029 (10% of 58 290 + 2000)**

Difference = GST payable. Does it reconcile with your GST account? **$1511**

Appendix C
Glossary

accounting the process of systematically recording, analysing and interpreting transactions.

accounting entity for accounting purposes, all businesses are considered to be separate entities from their owners. This means that the accounting records of the business must be kept separate from the owner's records. See also *legal entity*.

accounting process the systematic procedure for recording business transactions. See also *bookkeeping*.

accounting standards International Financial Reporting Standards (IFRS; pronounced if-er-us] as accepted by the Australian Accounting Standards Board. Usually these standards only apply to large or medium enterprises reporting to third parties, such as shareholders. See also *Tax Office standards*.

accounts payable a *general ledger* account that holds the total amount that we owe to our suppliers for inventory purchased on credit terms; also known as *trade payables* or *creditors control*. The individual accounts for each supplier are held in the creditors subsidiary ledger.

accounts receivable a *general ledger* account that holds the total amount that we are owed by our customers who have purchased inventory from us on credit terms; also known as *trade receivables* or *debtors control*. The individual accounts for each customer are held in the debtors subsidiary ledger.

accrual accounting all transactions are recorded when the contract is made, not when the amounts are settled. This is irrespective of whether or not it was a cash transaction and irrespective of the fact that the *GST* is creditable or due when the transaction is recorded. This can lead to cash flow problems for small businesses.

adjustment note a credit note issued by the supplier of goods or services, adjusting (usually reducing) the amount outstanding and also proportionally adjusting the *GST* component of the transaction.

assets items of value owned by the business and used by the business to earn revenue.

Australian Business Number (ABN) the business identifier allocated by the ATO. All businesses should register for an ABN even though they may not be required to register for the GST.

Australian Taxation Office (ATO) the government's principal revenue collection agency.

balance sheet a document showing in detail the assets, liabilities and owner's equity items at a particular time; shows the financial position of the business at this date.

bank reconciliation statement a report itemising the differences between the cash records of the business and those of the bank. After taking into account *unpresented cheques* and *unrecorded deposits*, the two records should agree.

bank statement a document prepared by the bank listing customers' use of their cheque accounts—for example, each deposit, presented cheque and automatic transfer.

bookkeeping the systematic recording of transactions by documents, journals and ledgers.

book value the historical cost of an asset (what you paid for it) less any accumulated depreciation.

borrowing costs the costs associated with the borrowing of money, but not including interest, such as the legal cost of writing up the mortgage contract. These are usually recorded as an expense under accounting standards and as an asset under the tax rules to be amortised over five years (or the length of the loan contract if shorter).

Business Activity Statement (BAS) the return that all businesses must lodge with the *ATO* monthly, quarterly or annually. It incorporates the *GST* return and records such tax liabilities as Pay As You Go (PAYG) withholding, PAYG income tax and fringe benefits tax (FBT).

capital the value of the owner's investment in the business.

capitalised costs an outlay of money that is recorded as an asset and then written off as an expense over time, usually in the form of depreciation.

cash not only means actual money, but in business usually means cheques and also includes direct debits and credit card transactions.

cash accounting under *ATO* rules this is more accurately modified cash accounting; that is, all assets and liabilities are recorded when the contract is made, irrespective of when the cash changes hands. However, for income and expense items, they are only recorded when you settle the account, irrespective of whether it was a cash or credit transaction.

cash at bank (CAB) money (cash, cheques, money orders, credit card sales and direct debits) deposited in the cheque account. All cash receipts should be banked intact and recorded in the cash receipts journal. All payments should be made by cheque or electronically (but never by cash) and recorded in the cash payments journal.

cash flow statement shows the source of cash used by the business, and the use to which that cash was put. The cash flow statement is the third member of the trilogy comprising balance sheet, income statement and cash flow statement.

chart of accounts a list of all the *general ledger* accounts coded and in order, a numerical index to the general ledger accounts.

company a business owned by a shareholder or shareholders; a separate *legal entity* from its owners.

consignment when goods are sent on consignment, the consignor retains ownership while the goods are waiting to be sold. The consignee stores the goods and presents them for sale. At the time of sale, ownership passes to the buyer; at no time does the consignee own the goods.

consumer a person who purchases a product or service for personal use; the last link in the distribution chain.

control account a *general ledger* account that summarises many transactions recorded in a subsidiary ledger. For example, the *creditors control* holds the monthly totals of the amounts posted to the creditors ledger and its balance is the balance outstanding of all creditors in the individual creditors' accounts.

cost of goods sold (COGS) see *cost of sales.*

cost of sales often referred to as *COGS*, this ledger classification holds the cost of inventory purchases, plus inwards freight, customs duties and any other costs incurred in getting your goods for resale delivered to your back door. When determining the annual profit, the *COGS* is adjusted to account for the movement in the inventory over the year.

credit an entry in a *general ledger* account that represents the economic outflows from a business transaction.

creditors account see *accounts payable.*

creditors control see *accounts payable.*

credit purchase a purchase of trading stock on credit terms; for example, 'Net 14 days'.

credit sale the sale of trading stock on credit terms.

current assets cash or other assets (such as *trading stock* or *trade debtors*) that are convertible to cash within one year.

current liabilities debts or other financial obligations payable within one year (such as *trade creditors*).

debit an entry in a *general ledger* account that represents the economic inflows from a business transaction.

debtors account see *accounts receivable.*

debtors control see *accounts receivable.*

decline in value *ATO* term used for *depreciation*. The rate of depreciation is determined by accounting standards whereas the decline in value is a tax-deductible amount determined by the ATO. Most *micro businesses* use the ATO decline in value amounts as their depreciable amounts.

depreciation the annual allocation of part of an asset's historical cost to an expense in recognition of its depleting value over time; see also *decline in value.*

dishonoured cheque a cheque presented to the bank but unable to be honoured, usually due to insufficient cash in the drawer's bank account.

double-entry bookkeeping the basic principle of recording the economic flow of business transactions for every debit entry (economic flow inwards) there must be an equivalent credit entry (economic flow outwards) in the *general ledger.*

drawings cash, stock or anything else of value that the owner takes out of the business for personal use.

franchise a business arrangement where, for an initial fee and usually an annual payment, a business may operate using a trademark or trade name and use knowledge and expertise provided by the franchisor.

general journal a journal used to record transactions for which a *special journal* is not suitable; see also *special journal.*

general ledger a collection of ledger accounts into which transactions are posted in total from journals; holds the details of business transactions of the same type.

goods and services tax (GST) a tax on goods and services sold within Australia. The tax is collected by the provider of the good or service and remitted to the *ATO* on a *BAS* form on a quarterly basis, net of any GST paid on purchases made by the provider.

GST free supplies, goods or services that are *GST* exempt, such as basic foodstuffs.

income statement see *profit and loss statement.*

incurred with regard to a business transaction, it is the time that the contract became binding and an amount of money is due, either now or in the future. It is at this point that transactions are normally recorded in your accounting records; however, for cash-based businesses this recording time is delayed until the account is actually settled.

input tax credit *GST* paid by a 'registered' purchaser on which the purchaser can claim a tax credit on their *BAS*.

International Financial Reporting Standards (IFRS) see *accounting standards* and *Tax Office standards*.

inventory the goods you purchase for resale at a profit. The purchase of inventory is debited to the Purchases account under *COGS*. The cost of inventory in your accounts is determined by your annual stocktake. See also *cost of sales*.

journal a summary of transactions that are first evidenced by business 'source' documents. The details on these documents are transferred to journals, such as the *general journal,* cash receipts journal, cash payments journal, purchases journal and sales journal, on a periodic, often daily, basis. The journals are totalled monthly and posted to the *general ledger*.

ledger account a record of each individual type of account, for example, an Electricity account or a Motor Vehicle account.

legal entity a legal concept identifying the possessor of legal rights and obligations, such as the ability to make contracts in its own name, obligation to pay debts or taxes, ability to initiate legal proceedings or be sued. As a contrast, see *accounting entity*.

micro business see *small business*.

net profit (loss) the difference between revenue earned and expenses incurred; profit (loss) = revenue less expenses.

noncurrent assets items of value that will not be exchanged for or converted to cash within the next 12 months, such as your business premises or motor vehicles.

noncurrent liabilities obligations that do not require payment within the next 12 months, such as a mortgage.

operating cycle the continuous flow of business transactions. Cash from sales comes into the business and is used to pay suppliers and other business expenses and buy more stock. When sold, the stock generates cash and so the cycle continues.

overdraft a loan from a financial institution made available through the cheque (trading) account. The business can continue to write cheques even though there are insufficient funds in the bank to cover them, up to an agreed value.

owner's equity the accounts classification that in total shows the net worth of the owner's investment in the business, often referred to as proprietorship.

partnership a business owned by two to 20 persons, each of whom is bound by the others' decisions and liable for all the debts of the business *(unlimited liability)*. Partnership structures are governed by the various state Partnership Acts.

partnership agreement a contract between partners of a business documenting each partner's rights, duties and liabilities.

posting the transferring of journal totals to the *general ledger* accounts.

profit and loss statement a document showing the revenues earned by a business and expenses incurred. Expenses are subtracted from revenues, leaving a net profit or loss. Also called an income statement or a *statement of financial performance*.

proprietary company a 'private' company registered with Australian Securities and Investments Commission (ASIC) owned by a shareholder or shareholders (maximum 50), with the words 'Proprietary Limited' (Pty Ltd) after its name.

proprietorship the value of the owner's property interest in the business, see also *owner's equity.*

public company usually a large company with the word 'Limited' (Ltd) after the name. It has the right to offer shares to the public at large and has no restrictions on the transfer of shares.

purchase order a document requesting a supplier to deliver specified items at a specified price; it is an offer to purchase, not a contract.

purchases expenses incurred in buying and trading stock for cash or on credit; in a cash-based business the purchase is recorded when the goods are actually paid for and not when the expense is incurred.

revenue money earned by a business. Trading businesses earn revenue from selling and trading stock, and service businesses by providing knowledge and skills for a fee.

revenue earned *revenue* that a business can legally record as revenue even though cash has not been received because a contract of sale has been concluded. Revenue is normally recognised when earned, not when received, but in cash-based businesses it is only recognised on receipt.

sales revenue income earned from selling and trading stock for cash or credit.

service business a business providing specialised knowledge and skills, such as medical, gardening or accounting businesses. Income earned is from fees.

small business defined by the *ATO* as a business with an annual turnover of less than $2 million. They are often referred to as micro businesses and account for their business transactions on a cash basis according to *ATO* rules.

small to medium enterprise (SME) a small business with a turnover in excess of $2 million but not more than $20 million. They account for their business transactions on an accrual basis under Australian accounting standards.

sole trader a business owned by one person who is liable for all debts of the business *(unlimited liability).*

special journals journals summarising one type of transaction; for example, the sales journal summarises credit sales of trading stock.

statement of financial performance alternative name for *profit and loss statement* or *income statement*.

statement of financial position alternative name for *balance sheet.*

stock the items a trading business buys and sells (trades in); also referred to as goods or trading stock. See also *inventory*.

stock in trade see *inventory.*

subsidiary ledger a ledger providing detail to support the *general ledger;* commonly used for *trade debtors, trade creditors, stock* and payroll. The *general ledger* includes summary accounts called control accounts, while the subsidiary ledgers record the full details for each debtor, creditor, stock item or employee.

sundry creditor a person or business to whom the business owes money as a result of purchasing an asset, such as a motor vehicle, other than trading stock on credit.

T account a precomputerisation ledger format where the left side of the 'T' records debit entries and the right records credit entries.

tax invoice an invoice issued by a 'registered' supplier of goods or services to the purchaser, indicating the amount of *GST* included in the purchase.

Tax Office standards the Income Tax Assessment Acts contain a number of concessionary rules in regard to *small businesses*. The Commissioner of Taxation, usually referred to as the Tax Office or the *ATO*, has issued a number of publications on the interpretation and application of these rules. It is by these rules, rather than the *IFRS*, that most small businesses abide. See also *accounting standards*.

trade creditor a person or business to which the business owes money for services or stock purchased on credit; see also *accounts payable*.

trade debtor a person or business that owes the business money for services or stock sold on credit; see also *accounts receivable*.

trade payables see *accounts payable*.

trade receivables see *accounts receivable*.

trading business a business that buys and sells trading stock (includes retailers and *wholesalers*).

trading name the name your business can trade under (provided that you have registered it with the appropriate state authority).

trading stock: see *inventory*.

transaction the exchange of goods or services that results in an obligation to pay or receive money.

trial balance a list of *general ledger* account balances; checks that debt balances equal credit balances.

turnover used as in small business turnover under $2 million; includes all ordinary income you earn in the ordinary course of business for the income year.

unlimited liability an obligation to pay business debts that is not limited to the value of business assets or the ownership percentage of the business and extends to the personal assets of investors.

unpresented cheques cheques that have been written by the business and sent to creditors, but have not been deposited into a bank account (presented) by the time the *bank statement* has been prepared.

unrecorded deposits deposits recorded in the business records but not recorded by the bank at the time the *bank statement* was prepared.

wholesaler a business that purchases stock from manufacturers, or their representatives and on-sells them to retailers (the middle man).

Index